"Stuart's Book Architecture M                      ry soul of my book. As we carefu                      er-ated, Stuart helped me sift the wheat from the chaff, identify series, flesh out the structure, and thus become aware of what the book really wanted to express. If my book helps readers it will be in great part because Stuart first helped me."

—Rev. Ed Bacon, author of *8 Habits of Love: Open Your Heart,*
*Open Your Mind* and frequent guest on Oprah Winfrey's Soul Series

"Refreshing, generous, demystifying, and inspiring, Horwitz's *Blueprint Your Bestseller* is the most practical and pleasurable piece of writing on writing I have ever read."

—Liza Ward, prize-winning author of *Outside Valentine*

"Stuart Horwitz's *Blueprint Your Bestseller* is a wonderful gift for any-one who has a book inside of him or her and wants to bring the words to life. By helping so many authors achieve their goals, Stu knows precisely how to guide and achieve this process for his readers. Plus, his book is as much fun and is just as kind to writers as he is."

—SaraKay Smullens, bestselling author of *Whoever Said Life Is Fair?*
and *Setting Yourself Free*

"The Book Architecture Method takes the precarious construction process of writing a manuscript and helps writers recognize the quality building blocks of their book. Complex storytelling ele-ments are broken down with an almost mathematical objectivity in a way that is effective for people who learn both visually and con-ceptually. *Blueprint Your Bestseller* is a great tool to have in the box."

—Nichole Bernier, author of *The Unfinished Work of Elizabeth D* and
finalist for the 2012 New England Independent Booksellers fiction award

*continued . . .*

"There has been no greater blessing during the process of writing my book than Stuart Horwitz of Book Architecture. His genius and humor gave me great encouragement and created clarity and structure for my book. Now those insights are contained in *Blueprint Your Bestseller*, reminding all writers that—in both work and life—unity is the highest good!"

—Vernā Myers, author of *Moving Diversity Forward: How to Go from Well-Meaning to Well-Doing*

"Self-help books about writing are usually crammed full of Virginia Woolf quotes and exclamation points, so imagine my surprise when I opened *Blueprint Your Bestseller*. My cynicism and trepidation morphed into the literary equivalent of shock and awe by page two. Stuart Horwitz had me scribbling notes in the margins of his indispensable book late into the night. *Blueprint Your Bestseller* is as inspiring as it is invaluable."

—Elizabeth Flock, *New York Times* bestselling author of *Me & Emma* and *What Happened to My Sister*

# Blueprint Your Bestseller

Organize and Revise Any Manuscript
with the Book Architecture Method

## STUART HORWITZ

A PERIGEE BOOK

**A PERIGEE BOOK**
**Published by the Penguin Group**
**Penguin Group (USA) Inc.**
**375 Hudson Street, New York, New York 10014, USA**

Penguin Group (Canada), 90 Eglinton Avenue East, Suite 700, Toronto, Ontario M4P 2Y3, Canada (a division of Pearson Penguin Canada Inc.) • Penguin Books Ltd., 80 Strand, London WC2R 0RL, England • Penguin Ireland, 25 St. Stephen's Green, Dublin 2, Ireland (a division of Penguin Books Ltd.) • Penguin Group (Australia), 707 Collins Street, Melbourne, Victoria 3008, Australia (a division of Pearson Australia Group Pty Ltd.) • Penguin Books India Pvt. Ltd., 11 Community Centre, Panchsheel Park, New Delhi—110 017, India • Penguin Group (NZ), 67 Apollo Drive, Rosedale, Auckland 0632, New Zealand (a division of Pearson New Zealand Ltd.) • Penguin Books (South Africa), Rosebank Office Park, 181 Jan Smuts Avenue, Parktown North 2193, South Africa • Penguin China, B7 Jiaming Center, 27 East Third Ring Road North, Chaoyang District, Beijing 100020, China

Penguin Books Ltd., Registered Offices: 80 Strand, London WC2R 0RL, England

While the author has made every effort to provide accurate telephone numbers, Internet addresses, and other contact information at the time of publication, neither the publisher nor the author assumes any responsibility for errors, or for changes that occur after publication. Further, the publisher does not have any control over and does not assume any responsibility for author or third-party websites or their content.

First edition: February 2013

Library of Congress Cataloging-in-Publication Data

Horwitz, Stuart.
Blueprint Your Bestseller: Organize and Revise Any Manuscript with the Book Architecture Method / Stuart Horwitz.—First Edition.
    pages    cm
Includes bibliographical references.
ISBN 978-0-399-16215-2
1. Authorship—Handbooks, manuals, etc.   2. Authorship—Vocational guidance.   3. Authorship—Marketing.   I. Title.
PN147.H656   2013
808.02—dc23                    2012037948

PRINTED IN THE UNITED STATES OF AMERICA

10  9  8  7  6  5  4  3

Most Perigee books are available at special quantity discounts for bulk purchases for sales promotions, premiums, fund-raising, or educational use. Special books, or book excerpts, can also be created to fit specific needs. For details, write: Special Markets, Penguin Group (USA) Inc., 375 Hudson Street, New York, New York 10014.

ALWAYS LEARNING                                                   PEARSON *it all goes back to Bonnie*

# Contents

# Theme, Part I

# Theme, Part II

# Series, Part II

# Scene, Part II

# Introduction

## The Book Architecture Method

The Book Architecture Method is a way of organizing and revising any manuscript that will get you from first draft to final draft. Maybe you started writing on a whim and got to page 100 or 200 of a book-length project before your efforts started to stall; you do not need a complete manuscript to benefit from the Book Architecture Method. Maybe you have 435 pages of something you've been revising for years. Either way, your material can benefit from the sequential action steps presented here. Time and again I have heard writers say that this method helps them "tackle their work, as opposed to tinker with it." With a framework and a focus, it is possible to dispel any fog that may surround your work in progress and rekindle your excitement for something you thought might be tangled and dreaded. My goal is simply to help you work on your book with direction.

Because the method is not prescriptive about content, it can be applied to fiction; to narrative nonfiction, such as memoir; and across media to theater, film, and TV. Even writers of traditional nonfiction have found great value in the three main concepts of the Book Architecture Method: how to present their material in *scene*, through the repetition and variation of *series*, and in the service of one central *theme*.* By visiting the three main concepts— scene, series, and theme—once in that order, and then a second time in reverse order, you will be able to rework your entire manuscript in a far more powerful way. You will still need to go back and clean up minor issues—but your narrative architecture will be sound.

I call what follows here a method and not a formula, because its value comes when it is applied to your work on its own terms. It isn't like baking, where you're going to add a certain amount of suspense or a dash of introspection at a particular time. Some books do that, but I prefer not to be so prescriptive. What you choose to write about is your business. How to help it mean the most it can to your readers is what this book is about.

Of course you will need some pages to get started, maybe between 80 and 120. One hundred fifty pages is even better.† This may seem arbitrary, but I have worked with writers who had only 65 pages and they felt like they couldn't get the most out of the method, and I don't want this to happen to you. If you need a few more pages, turn to the next section and read "How to Generate Material." That's Action Step Zero.

---

\* Another way of saying this? This book you're reading right now is traditional nonfiction, and it was written using the method.

† For the sake of this book, we'll take a page to be around 250 words, so 80 to 120 pages = 20,000 to 30,000 words.

After that, the method gets under way in earnest, with twenty-two action steps described in great detail. Twenty-two may seem like a big number. Really, the number you need to know is three: scene, series, and theme. With the exception of scene, you may not be used to hearing these terms in writing circles. Terms you would expect to see in a book on writing, such as *plot* and *point of view*, I use rarely, if at all. Some terms, such as *character*, are used, but only in a specific sense. What writers are taught in general leans heavily in the direction of how to express content rather than how we might structure our work to communicate with the reader. Scene, series, and theme help us to see better what is going on at the structural level.

Some initial definitions of our three major terms, then:

- **Scene:** A scene is a group of self-contained passages within your narrative. Putting all of your material into one scene or another can help you move scenes around, divide and combine them, and eliminate them when necessary. Scenes are the building blocks of your work. This expands on the traditional definition of *scene*, which is generally used to indicate the dramatic parts of a narrative only. In this method, everything belongs to one scene or another.

- **Series:** Anything that repeats and varies in your work can be considered a series: a character as he or she evolves, a relationship that has its ups and downs, an object that becomes a symbol. The repetitions and variations in a series can be traced as they develop. This is what is known as the *narrative arc*.

- **Theme:** The theme is the central conflict or concept of your work, its thesis. Your theme is the one thing that your book is about because your book can only be about one thing. Seems easy enough, right?

Scene, series, and theme are all concepts that we will come back to throughout this book. We will build on their definitions. I know you would like to know everything at once, but trust me, it's better to ease into things. You can always go to the Glossary in the back when you want the full definition of a term, or when you simply want to meditate on a particular concept for a little while.

Okay, enough meditating. We have work to do. The work of organization and revision is like climbing a mountain: It can be strenuous in parts, but there are beautiful vistas. Chapters One to Ten follow this journey up and down the mountain.

We begin in "Scene, Part I," establishing the boundaries of your scenes (since everything will go with either one scene or another) while we get an initial read on what you love about your book and what still needs work. Here we consider not only what you still want to write but also how you can start attacking your present work to get ready for your next draft. After this, we move to "Series, Part I," examining your scenes more closely to find what repeats and varies. The places where you have returned to things that interest you are the birthplaces of your series, where

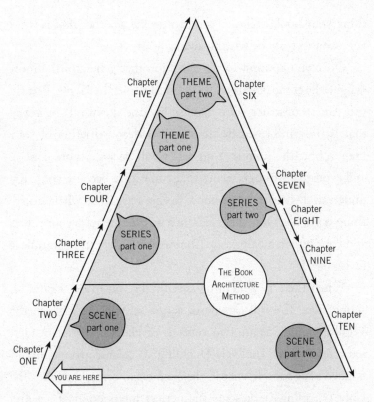

The Book Architecture Method, just starting out.

you will find the heart of your work. It is through your series that you communicate what your theme is, which is the focus of the next section, "Theme, Part I," the top of the mountain.

Understanding what you have created to this point is one side of the mountain; the other side—and the view from the top—is explored in the next section, "Theme, Part II." Like climbing a mountain, it is far less interesting if you hike down the same way you came up. After you discover your theme, the one thing your book is about, you can decide whether that is what you want to truly be writing about.

Once you commit to the direction that generates the most delight, the climb down gets progressively easier. In "Series, Part II" you can reconstruct your manuscript (the downhill) in a way that is fully informed by the previous deconstruction of your manuscript (the uphill). Your series will become more concise and evocative through scenes that come alive because you truly understand their purpose now. "Scene, Part II" is where everything is put back together again in a way that reflects your values and your intent; a base camp from which to depart for your next revision.

When there is something specific for you to do, I offer an action step. The full catalog of action steps is available in the "Tools" section, as are two versions of Hans Christian Andersen's short story "The Ugly Duckling" (a clean copy and an annotated copy for reference in the chapters to come). I think "The Ugly Duckling" represents the perfect intersection of art and science, even though some students have protested against my using this short story as the chief example of the method. Like them, you may find it corny and overly moralistic, with a questionable conclusion (one's pedigree is all that determines one's worth). I really just want us to have a common reference text, but a good class is always controversial.

Speaking of students: Many people have helped the method evolve to this point either by being brilliant clients or by belonging to the savvy group I have taught at Grub Street, a nonprofit creative writing center in Boston. I refer to many of these individuals by their first names in the work that follows. The experience of working with talented individuals who give you feedback (known in this book as *beta readers*) can be invaluable—provided that your readers have the same framework and focus you are striving to develop. To this end, I have included a Guide for Beta Readers in the "Tools" section that can be either used in an active workshop or adapted for use with an individual beta reader.

As the social psychologist Kurt Lewin once remarked, "There is nothing so practical as a good theory." In that spirit, I must ask you one favor. When the desire to write seizes you while reading this book—to craft a new scene whose possibilities announce themselves to your imagination, or to reinvest in a shaky scene with renewed sparkle and purpose—please put the book down and do so. Planning such as this gives you questions—more refined questions, perhaps—but it is only the writing itself that will give you any answers. This method is designed to invite a collaboration with active writing. Inspiring you to write—and to finish what you write—is this book's only purpose.

# How to Generate Material

## Action Step Zero

You should always be writing. It is in the writing that you will find the answers to the questions this method poses. It is also how you get better. Sometimes we labor under the mistaken assumption that our talent as a writer is static. Either you got talent or you didn't—and if you did, you got a certain amount of it, no more. If that is true, then writing stands alone among human endeavors as something you cannot get appreciably better at with practice.

As I mentioned in the introduction, to get the most out of the method you will need approximately 100 pages of a first draft if you are working on a book-length manuscript. The prompts that follow are designed to help you generate the material necessary to use the Book Architecture Method. Even if you are an old hand at writing, someone who has written a full draft and maybe even a previous book or several articles, this chapter may remind you of some helpful approaches you have temporarily forgotten. Maybe you will have outgrown some of these suggestions—if so, good for you . . . and I mean it! You have most likely developed your own process for facing the great unknown of the blank page. This is mine.

## 1. Count Your Words

It seems so anal, I know. But I count every word I write, even if the words are handwritten. Word-processing programs make this easy: highlight the new passages, get your count. Why do we count words religiously? For two reasons: It helps us understand the nature of a first draft, and it helps us reach our goals.

Let's take the nature of a first draft. When you are generating material for a first draft, each word you write is as good as every other word. Hard to believe, I know. Empirically untrue, even. Yet from one angle this is the gospel, because you cannot simultaneously generate new material and know its true value. To do so would be to time-travel into the future, to be able to look back with the measuring mind at the same time you are using the creative mind. It's not possible. So we must accept that we don't know where these words are going . . . and that to evaluate them will cause their flow to stop.

When we are generating material, we just write. We count words in lieu of being able to say whether what we are writing is any good. Since we can't know that yet, we have to set another kind of goal: ten thousand words in a month, for example. "That seems so easy!" you might say. "That's only twenty-five hundred words a week—less than four pages each time I write, if I write three times a week. I can easily do more than that!"

Yes, but many people aren't writing that much, currently. No offense. That may be because they are trying to get to fifty thousand words in one afternoon. We purposely set the goal a little low because it's not about wearing yourself out. It's about finding your pace. Life will get in the way, and if you have set the bar just a little bit low, you can handle unforeseen obstacles to your day or week and still produce ten thousand words in a month.* After five months, you will have written fifty thousand words— have a glass of champagne for me! After two and a half more months, you will have enough to begin this method in earnest.

---

**Remember:** *Ten thousand words a month. They don't have to be good.*

---

## 2. Find a Neutral Audience

The minute you start writing things down, things get complicated. The question "Is it good enough?" morphs into "Am I good enough?"—and a temporary ceasing of the word flow is sure to follow. I don't know about you, but when I feel backed into a corner, I turn to the people I think are rooting for me (we'll call them the *cheerleaders*); I try to use their positive

---

* I call it "the 10K challenge."

energy to blot out any negative energy I may encounter from harsh or careless sources (we'll call them the *critics*). But that doesn't always work in the end. The more I try to embrace one group, the more I find myself face-to-face with the other group.

Better to find a neutral audience to write to. Whereas a critic might say what you are working on has been done before, that you are working in a crowded field, a neutral audience member might say, "Let's see." Whereas your cheerleaders might tell you they've never heard anything like your story, your neutral audience just wants to hear it for themselves.

Your neutral audience may not be anybody you will ever meet. They don't need you to be too self-deprecating, but they don't want a bunch of ego, either. They just want the information. If it's nonfiction, they're wondering, "What do I need to know about this?" If it's fiction, they want to know what happens next.

You might find a neutral audience member in a writing workshop. You might hire an independent editor (ahem). You might read the riot act to one of your close friends and say, "Look, I don't want you to tell me that you love it, and I don't want you to tell me that you're not my audience (i.e., you hate it). I want you to be neutral; you can do it."

When we can write to someone neutral, we enter this balanced place, through a portal that is life-giving. You think it might be kind of a bland experience, but it's not. It's a whole other universe.

---

**Remember:** *If you don't know whether what you're writing is any good, why not write to someone who doesn't know, either?*

---

## 3. Don't Try to Organize Anything

This stems from the idea that you don't know what's of value while you are writing a first draft—so you certainly don't know where it goes. The freedom that comes from putting everything into one long document is pretty amazing, if you can embrace it. With the *Edit > Find* feature on our computers, we can find any passage later with only a keyword. (If you can't remember the correct keyword, chances are you don't need to find what you think you are looking for.)

In this one long document, you may find yourself repeating things—that's actually good. These repetitions and variations will form your series, one of the core concepts of the Book Architecture Method. Repeating yourself is good because it means you are trying to get at the heart of what you really want to say.

Eventually we will sift through all of the material you have generated to find the organizing principles: your scenes, your series, and your theme. First drafts can be messy, dense thickets of material, but they need be wild only once. As long as your draft covers the ground, gives us some who, what, where, and when, then the method can work on the why—and whip the rest of your material up into a frenzy. That's the work of organization and revision: taking the best parts seriously.

Let's not get ahead of ourselves, however. Some clients are so relieved when I tell them that all they have to do at this stage is write fifty pages of crap. "I wrote fifty pages of crap!" they announce proudly. "What do I do next?" Write another fifty pages of crap. Then you will have a hundred pages of crap.

But it won't be all crap. Your really good material will be nestled inside what you have created, and I will train your eye to see its inner glow. Sometimes it will be obvious. I remember reviewing one afternoon's writing and finding a poem that needed virtually no editing. I told myself I was just typing words and hitting the return key—but there it was between lines twelve and twenty-six.

The appearance of the good stuff will always be unexpected. In the meantime you can do only one draft at a time. If you're generating first-draft material and you're not writing like the wind, then that's nothing more than perfectionism. Write quickly, with no "backspacing," as the kids say these days; write illogically, without concern for punctuation or word choice. And above all, don't look back. If you do, you will be like Lot's wife, who turned to a pillar of salt when she gazed backward—a great metaphor for writer's block. What is there to see back there, exactly, anyway? What you screwed up? It will still be there, believe me.

Remember: *One draft at a time.*

## 4. Make the Time

We're all busy. I hear writers worry that they cannot maintain their momentum because they are juggling so many things: a sick parent, a full-time job, a stab at a social life—I know the feeling. How am I going to write this book, coach a bunch of ungrateful teenagers in softball, keep up the integrity of my work as an independent editor, be a good father to kid number two, do the grocery shopping and my own laundry because that is where the wife draws the line . . . you get the picture.

So you and I, we have an absolute ton to do. But writing is on the list, right? Because if writing doesn't even *make* the list, then we have a different kind of problem. We need to solve that one first. If you are struggling to justify the importance of your writing, if you are listening to negative value judgments about being a good enough writer or worrying about why you're not doing something more productive like making widgets, then you aren't going to be able to make the time.

Assuming we've made it through those psychological hurdles, and we really do want to make the time, then we need to take a flexible—perhaps unconventional—approach to scheduling. As Keith Richards* said about another of our rigid patterns, eating:

> We've been trained from babyhood to have three square meals a day, the full factory-industrial revolution of how you're supposed to eat. Before then it was never like that. When the hooter goes, you eat.†

The same can be said about our writing schedule. Why don't we write from nine p.m. to two a.m., sleep for four hours, wake up and deal with the kids and all of the details, then go back to sleep for four more hours?

---

\* Hey, you can't always quote Saul Bellow.

† P.S. *Hooter* is British slang for "nose."

Maybe your body doesn't work that way, but I think it's worthwhile to ask questions about how you do operate. Personally, I find it useful to have a long block of hours in which to write, even if that means that I don't get to write as often, and there's a touch more pressure on those days for being fewer. I want to go for a run first, or take a nap, or maybe both. I want the day to be able to take its own pace and not have anything pressing at the end, either. Sometimes this means working on the weekends. Sometimes it means saying no to social obligations. Whatever your life conditions are, you can apply the flexible approach to time management and create a schedule that works for you—fueling this flexibility with respect for your writing.

---

**Remember:** *You aren't a writer because you are published. You are a writer because you make time to write (and because you write your heart out).*

---

## 5. Listen

This is a big one. My friend is an energy healer, and she says that only 2 percent of what we think actually comes from our authentic selves. The rest of it is programming—you know, our culture or our faith or our family put a pinball in motion, and now it's just binging and clinking off every available surface in our minds.

Maybe you don't think my source is reputable. That's fine,

but let's consider the idea that it is. How would that help explain why writers struggle to find their voice? Isn't that the same kind of pinballing process, bouncing off authors we have treasured, getting hit by the flipper of self-doubt?

What if we pulled ourselves up from this proto–video game? What would we hear in our heads when we left the arcade? This is a hard thing to describe, but it sounds like your voice, the one you speak with. The irony of discovering something that was there all along is strange; I'll grant you that. When we do hear it, it may sound pretty sweet—but how do we tune in to our voice?

The answer, as you may have guessed, is to *stop thinking* and *start listening*. Saul Bellow* called it our prompter:

> I suppose that all of us have a primitive prompter or commentator within, who from earliest years has been advising us, telling us what the real world is. There is such a commentator in me. I have to prepare the ground for him. From this source come words, phrases, syllables; sometimes only sounds, which I try to interpret, sometimes whole paragraphs, fully punctuated.

Maybe you will object that you are not Saul Bellow. But by his definition, every one of us has a prompter. That's not the part of the equation we have to focus on; it's how do we prepare the ground for him or her? We might meditate, we might *make more time* to connect with this prompter before we even begin writing.

---

\* There he is!

We might localize this prompter in an icon or image and practice devotion to it—hey, stranger things have happened.

---

Remember: *Whatever prewriting rituals you choose, they should have this as their goal: fostering a willingness to listen.*

---

## 6. Have Fun

This one is pretty basic. If you've made the time to write, if you've set the date for your next writing session—and because you keep your appointments, it has arrived—why spend any time worrying about your chores while you are writing, or your bank account, or tomorrow's schedule? You've already committed to today, right? Isn't life to be enjoyed?

As Thoreau said, "What am I doing in the woods, if I am thinking of something out of the woods?" Thoreau wasn't exactly the master of fun, I'll grant you. Besides, everybody's definition of fun is different. Does having fun mean that you drink while you write? I don't know. I did, and then I didn't. Do you listen to music?

Do you bring some notes to your writing session—not too many, just enough to act as a kind of guide while you practice going off the deep end? And when we do this pre-planning about what we might write about, do we settle on something we are interested in, that we might actually enjoy?

I had an experience while writing this book that reminded me of this lesson. I was all prepared to write an appendix on the

Book Architecture Method and film. I had taught good classes on the material; I was on a writing retreat (*make the time*, check) and had brought the two films and one TV show I wanted to feature with me. But every time I looked over at the portable DVD player my youngest daughter had supplied me with, I felt irritated. It was going to be drudgery—maybe it would be right another time, but right now it would be joyless, pure execution.

So you know what? I didn't even try to write it. I took the idea for this essay, "How to Generate Material," out on the town instead, stopping at different coffee shops and street corners to write a few hundred words at a time. Now that was fun: switching up the music, letting it come, saying something that I agreed with, something that was new for me. I didn't want that day to end, I tell ya. I'm striving to follow my own advice and I mean it: Writing should be fun.

---

Remember: *There is fun to be had. It is up to you to have it.*

---

# Scene,
# Part I

# Chapter One

# What Is a Scene?

The basic premise of the Book Architecture Method is this: Your book has ninety-nine scenes. If you find your scenes and put them in the right order, you will be all set. I don't believe this is easier said than done—or harder said than done. It is what it is. There will be periods of questioning and there will be periods of joy; there will be divine inspiration searing across the page like a cosmic flame, and there will be fidgeting with things until they fit just right. All I can say is that it does happen. I have seen writers line up their ninety-nine scenes in the right order. When they do, the rest is just details.

When you start offering methods to people, their first question is, "Does it work?" As I mentioned in the introduction, this is a method, not a formula; as such, it needs to be applied. Does your book have exactly 99 scenes? I doubt it! Your book has 72 scenes, or 138 scenes, or another number that you won't know until you are done. I chose ninety-nine for the sake of discussion.

I chose it because it feels one shy of completion. You cannot achieve unity, the goal of any piece of writing,* by trying to be comprehensive. No matter how hard you try, you will never completely cover your topic—all you can do is be consistent and coherent. Perfectionism can appear in many guises, but it is always an impossible task that likes to present itself as something that isn't. We need to adjust our definition of perfection to mean "getting your ninety-nine scenes in the right order"—and let the hundredth come when it is good and ready.

## What Is a Scene?

Since we are trying to get our ninety-nine scenes in the right order, we need to first ask, "What is a scene?" Everything needs to be presented in a scene. The most commonly heard expression in writing circles is probably "Show, don't tell," which means you must put us in the scene. Don't tell us about it, don't tell us that it happened, don't tell us that your characters—or you as the narrator—had this set of feelings about it; make it happen for us as readers or viewers. The earliest reference to "Show, don't tell" is in Aristotle's *Poetics*:

> While constructing plots and working them out complete with their linguistic expression, one should so far as possible

---

* This is a large claim, but I am not the first to make it. "Unity is a fundamental—quite possibly the fundamental—aesthetic criterion" (*The New Princeton Encyclopedia of Poetry and Poetics*).

visualize what is happening. By envisaging things very vividly in this way, as if one were actually present at the events themselves, one can find out what is appropriate, and inconsistencies are least likely to be overlooked.

Scenes are how dramatic information is received. There are times to tell as well as show, of course, and I will return to this material in Chapter Ten. Even good telling, though, is embodied in a time and a place, with an emotion a reader and writer can share.

Two related definitions of scene have some currency these days. A scene is where something happens, and because something happens, something changes in a way that propels the narrative. In our work on series, we will examine how these changes can be charted and reconstructed in a rhythmic way that is capable of conveying meaning. For now, just remember:

**A scene is where something happens.**

**A scene is where something changes.**

There will eventually be five related definitions of scene, but we're on a need-to-know basis here. So let me just add one more at present:

**A scene is related to the central theme of the book.**

Because your book can only be about one thing, each scene has to relate to that one thing—your theme—in some way. Of course, at this stage of your work, you may not know what your one thing is—in fact, you probably don't, and that's okay. When I teach a class, for example, I have writers record what their theme is in week one; when they return to their original idea weeks later, they are always surprised and sometimes astounded by how their perception of their own work has changed by using this method. You can try this now: Write out a few sentences in answer to this question: "What is your book about?" This is not the same thing as "What happens in your book?" A lot happens in your book, I'm sure. But what is it about? This book is about a method for organization and revision. "The Ugly Duckling" is about a case of mistaken identity that reveals a variety of prejudices. What is the one thing your book is about?

## Scenes in "The Ugly Duckling"

Since we are all just starting up this mountain, I find it useful for us to have a narrative to study in common. Hence, "The Ugly Duckling." If you have not read "The Ugly Duckling" lately, please turn to the clean copy on page 167 and do so now. You will get so much more out of what follows.

Because developing an understanding of what a scene is will come in so handy when we examine our own manuscripts, the first exercise is to identify the number of scenes in "The Ugly Duckling." Flip to the clean copy in the "Tools" section, and by applying the first two definitions of scene (a scene is where something happens; a scene is where because something happens, something else changes), try to divide this story into its component scenes yourself.

There are a few tricks to use as you try to decide whether a certain set of passages belongs to the same scene, or if we are in an appreciably different part of the book.

**Scenes often occur in a single time period.**

**Scenes often occur in the same place.**

**Scenes often have one central subject matter.**

These diagnostics are based on Aristotle's three unities: a play should operate in a single place, it should depict a limited time period (either twenty-four or thirty-six hours), and all of the events presented should contribute to a single action (or, in our case, your book can only be about one thing). While the unities proved a little restrictive for an entire work of drama, I think they can be applied profitably to individual scenes. Keep these three ideas in mind when you look at the individual scenes in "The Ugly Duckling," and they will help you track where one scene ends and the next scene begins.

Are you ready with your number of scenes in "The Ugly Duckling"? Six is a number I feel I can defend. I have attended many lively conversations about why this short story could have thirty-two scenes or seventeen scenes, or perhaps more reasonably, nine scenes. The reason why well-intentioned writers have lobbied for nine scenes instead of six may be due to the fact that the links are so skillful. A link is a passage, from a single phrase to several pages in length, that moves the reader from one scene to the next. (Links can be unobtrusive or they can be obvious; Chapter Ten will discuss varieties of links.)

Consider the following passage:

"Well, if we don't understand you, who should? I suppose you don't consider yourself cleverer than the cat or the old woman, not to mention me! Don't make a fool of yourself, child, and thank your stars for all the good we have done you. Have you not lived in this warm room, and in such society that you might have learned something? But you are an idiot, and there is no pleasure in associating with you. You may believe me: I mean you well. I tell you home truths, and there is no surer way than that of knowing who are one's friends. You just set about laying some eggs, or learn to purr, or to emit sparks."

"I think I will go out into the wide world," said the duckling.

"Oh, do so by all means," said the hen.

*(end scene four)*

---

*(begin scene five)*

So away went the duckling. He floated on the water and ducked underneath it, but he was looked at askance and was slighted by every living creature for his ugliness. Now autumn came. The leaves in the woods turned yellow and brown. The wind took hold of them, and they danced about.

The sky looked very cold and the clouds hung heavy with snow and hail. A raven stood on the fence and croaked "Caw, caw!" from sheer cold. It made one shiver to think of it. The poor duckling certainly was in a bad case!

-----------------------------------------------------------------

One evening, the sun was just setting in wintry splendor when a flock of beautiful large birds appeared out of the bushes. The duckling had never seen anything so beautiful. They were dazzlingly white with long waving necks. They were swans, and uttering a peculiar cry they spread out their magnificent broad wings and flew away from the cold regions to warmer lands and open seas . . .

The link, the middle paragraph presented here, binds scenes four and five together as if it were mortar between two bricks. I have drawn a bold line to separate the two scenes where I have because it has to go somewhere, but I could also have drawn it where the dashed line is. If you cannot tell which scene a link belongs to, that is the sign of a successful link. When it comes to dividing your own scenes, which you will do at the end of the next chapter, you can put the link with whichever passage makes marginally more sense.

Once we become aware of the potential challenges posed by some links, we can return to the three unities of scene (scenes occur in a single time period, in the same place, and have one subject) and find that dividing a narrative into its component parts is really not that difficult.

"Let me look at the egg which won't crack," said the old duck. "You may be sure that it is a turkey's egg! I was cheated like that once and I had no end of trouble and worry with the creatures, for I may tell you that they are afraid of the water. I simply could not get them into it. I quacked and snapped at them, but it all did no good. Let me see the egg! Yes, it is a turkey's egg. You just leave it alone, and teach the other children to swim."

"I will sit on it a little longer. I have sat so long already that I may as well go on till the Midsummer Fair comes round."

"Please yourself," said the old duck, and away she went.

At last the big egg cracked. "Cheep, cheep!" said the young one and tumbled out. How big and ugly he was! The duck looked at him.

"That is a monstrous big duckling," she said. "None of the others looked like that. Can he be a turkey chick? Well, we shall soon find that out. Into the water he shall go, if I have to kick him in myself."

*(end scene one)*

---

*(begin scene two)*

Next day was gloriously fine, and the sun shone on all the great dock leaves. The mother duck with her whole family went down to the moat.

Splash! into the water she sprang. "Quack, quack," she said, and one duckling plumped in after the other. The water dashed over their heads, but they came up again and floated beautifully. Their legs went of themselves, and they were all there. Even the big ugly gray one swam about with them.

"No, that is no turkey," she said. "See how beautifully he uses his legs and how erect he holds himself. He is my own chick, after all, and not bad looking when you come to look at him properly. Quack, quack! Now come with me and I will take you out into the world and introduce you to the duckyard. But keep close to me all the time so that no one will tread upon you. And beware of the cat!"

The separation between scene one and two above is relatively easy to detect, because of the time shift. Sometimes a link can be a paragraph or longer, as we saw before; sometimes it can be a simple phrase. "Next day was gloriously fine." That's it. The setting and characters remain the same, which allows the action to develop in a comprehensible way, because we are familiar with the surroundings. There is also a time shift that signals the transition from scene two to scene three provided by the simple link, "So the first day passed."

"The other ducklings are very pretty," said the old duck. "Now make yourselves quite at home, and if you find the head of an eel you may bring it to me."

After that they felt quite at home. But the poor duckling who had been the last to come out of the shell, and who was so ugly, was bitten, pushed about, and made fun of both by the ducks and the hens. "He is too big," they all said. And the turkey cock, who was born with his spurs on and therefore thought himself quite an emperor, puffed himself up like a vessel in full sail, made for him, and gobbled and gobbled till he became quite red in the face. The poor duckling did not know which way to turn. He was in despair because he was so ugly and the butt of the whole duckyard.

*(end scene two)*

---

*(begin scene three)*

So the first day passed, and afterwards matters grew worse and worse. The poor duckling was chased and hustled by all of them. Even his brothers and sisters ill-used him. They were always saying, "If only the cat would get hold of you, you hideous object!" Even his mother said, "I wish to goodness you were miles away." The ducks bit him, the hens pecked him, and the girl who fed them kicked him aside.

Then he ran off and flew right over the hedge, where the little birds flew up into the air in a fright.

"That is because I am so ugly," thought the poor duckling, shutting his eyes, but he ran on all the same. Then he came to a great marsh where the wild ducks lived. He was so tired and miserable that he stayed there the whole night. In the morning the wild ducks flew up to inspect their new comrade.

So far, so good. But now, in addition to a time shift, there is a change in the quality of time. In scene three, time speeds up—instead of lasting a single day like scenes one and two, it lasts for an indeterminate period. Once the basic coordinates of your story have been established, you too can begin to play with the expansion or compression of time, a switch in scenic locations, or a shift in subject matter. A change in location can be a very useful tool for identifying where one scene shifts to another. Scene two, for example, takes place under the "great dock leaves" while scene three happens in a marsh.

A change in setting also marks the separation between scene three and scene four:

"Oh, thank Heaven!" sighed the duckling. "I am so ugly that even the dog won't bite me!"

Then he lay quite still while the shots whistled among the bushes, and bang after bang rent the air. It only became quiet late in the day, but even then the poor duckling did not dare to get up. He waited several hours more before he looked about, and then he hurried away from the marsh as fast as he could. He ran across fields and meadows, and there was such a wind that he had hard work to make his way.

*(end scene three)*

---

*(begin scene four)*

Towards night he reached a poor little cottage. It was such a miserable hovel that it could not make up its mind which way even to fall, and so it remained standing. The wind whistled so fiercely around the duckling that he had to sit on his tail to resist it, and it blew harder and ever harder. Then he saw that the door had fallen off one hinge and hung so crookedly that he could creep into the house through the crack, and so he made his way into the room.

An old woman lived here with her cat and her hen. The cat, whom she called "Sonnie," would arch his back, purr, and give off electric sparks if you stroked his fur the wrong way. The hen had quite tiny short legs, and so she was called "Chickie low legs." She laid good eggs, and the old woman was as fond of her as if she had been her own child.

In the morning the strange duckling was discovered immediately, and the cat began to purr and the hen to cluck.

The final scenic division of the story occurs between scene five and scene six. Between scenes five and six, the time changes, the place changes, and the central action changes. The whole vibe changes, and you have a scene that is not only formally different—it is essentially different from the scene that precedes it. This is possible because of a special kind of link (explored in Chapter Ten) called a "voice-over" link. Basically, the voice-over link is a move by the narrator to change a variety of the coordinates of the story simply by telling us that is what is going to happen. I have placed this link in bold in the following passage:

Early in the morning a peasant came along and saw him. He went out onto the ice and hammered a hole in it with his heavy wooden shoe, and carried the duckling home to his wife. There he soon revived. The children wanted to play with him, but the duckling thought they were going to ill-use him, and rushed in his fright into the milk pan, and the milk spurted out all over the room. The woman shrieked and threw up her hands. Then he flew into the butter cask, and down into the meal tub and out again. Just imagine what he looked like by this time! The woman screamed and tried to hit him with the tongs. The children tumbled over one another in trying to catch him, and they screamed with laughter. By good luck the door stood open, and the duckling flew out among the bushes and the newly fallen snow. And he lay there thoroughly exhausted.

**But it would be too sad to mention all the privation and misery he had to go through during the hard winter.** When the sun began to shine warmly again, the duckling was in the marsh, lying among the rushes. The larks were singing and the beautiful spring had come.

*(end scene five)*

---

*(begin scene six)*

Then all at once he raised his wings and they flapped with much greater strength than before and bore him off vigorously.

Before he knew where he was, he found himself in a large garden where the apple trees were in full blossom and the air was scented with lilacs, the long branches of which overhung the indented shores of the lake. Oh, the spring freshness was delicious!

Just in front of him he saw three beautiful white swans advancing towards him from a thicket. With rustling feathers they swam lightly over the water. The duckling recognized the majestic birds, and he was overcome by a strange melancholy.

Now that we have separated Andersen's individual scenes from each other, the next step is to give each a name. Naming your own scenes will prove especially useful during the editing process when you are moving scenes around and evaluating them each on its own terms. A good name reflects the definitions of a scene: what happens, what changes, and how it relates to the theme. A good name will instantly bring you back to what that scene is about.

In "The Ugly Duckling" I have assigned the following names to the six scenes:

1. The Shell Will Not Crack
2. Can't Make Him Over
3. What Sort of a Creature Are You?
4. Conversation in the Cottage
5. The Hard Winter
6. The Royal Birds

Before we leave our scenic analysis of "The Ugly Duckling," I want to make one other observation about this story: the scenes are all almost exactly the same length. Scenes one through six are, respectively, 645 words, 742 words, 599 words, 693 words, 626 words, and 514 words. While this no doubt contributes to the rhythm of the story, such uniformity in scenic length is not necessary—or even very common. Sometimes a flashback scene can be done really well in a paragraph, and there are examples in literature where scenes are more than a hundred pages long.*

The important thing to understand is that a scene is not the same thing as a chapter. A chapter is a movement larger than a scene. There are also movements that are smaller than a scene; for example, a paragraph, a sentence, or a word. In fact, we will be taking all of our material out of chapters for now; in the Book Architecture Method, a scene is the basic measuring unit by which you will construct your manuscript. When these units are identified, they immediately become distinct. They are then mobile and flexible. They can be seen as weak or strong, as a hopeless aside, or as the climactic scene after all. They can be put in a different order getting a very different result. They are what unity is truly made of:

unit + unit + unit + unit = unity

Grasping the scene as a unit will orient you through your material in a way that nothing else can.

---

* In *Narrative Discourse*, Gérard Genette describes five scenes from Marcel Proust's *Remembrance of Things Past* that combined total almost 450 pages.

## Brainstorm Your Scenes

We are now ready for your first action step: making a list of all of your scenes . . . with a catch. You will keep this list throughout the process, so you may want to write it in a convenient place. In the future you will be highlighting scenes that need to be improved, adding the names of scenes you want to write, and saying good-bye to "bad" scenes once and for all. You will eventually use this list to reorder your scenes as you complete your organization and set yourself up for a successful revision.

For now, all you need to do is generate the list. When you list your scenes, include every scene you can think of, even the scenes that are not completely finished. Some may exist only in your mind. You may have a set of really good ideas that are still only sketched out in the briefest form, or you may have rewritten a scene several times. Through this process you will start to understand what a scene means to you and how it can best be detected in your writing.

The only rule is this: You cannot peek at the book itself. That's the catch! Make your list over a few days from memory only. Some scenes may come back to you in different physical environments you travel through, and that's great—keep the list with you as a reminder of your involvement with the narrative as a whole. You may feel that you will be able to remember every scene in your book. You won't. When you finish your list, you will find that you have forgotten scenes that are repetitive, tangential, or lacking any real impact. That is why it is imperative that the list be made from memory, because memory is the surest guide to the memorable—and the memorable is the surest guide to the meaningful.

**Action Step #1: Brainstorm Your Scenes**

Make a list of every scene in your book without looking at your manuscript. Give each scene a name that will bring you quickly back to what happens there.

# Chapter Two

# Ninety-Nine Good Scenes in the Right Order

After you made your list of scenes in the previous chapter, you may have realized something funny about them—there aren't ninety-nine! If there are, you did it wrong. You may have 117, or 54, or 136 and you aren't even close to through yet. Wouldn't it be great if you could know exactly how many scenes your manuscript had, as on a puzzle box?

"Then, you could pick out all the straight edges, and start with them," Maura pointed out in class. Maura was married to a statistician who wanted us all to know that life is a series of "successive approximations." Meaning, you get close, and then you get closer. Maybe right now you have eighty-six scenes—at least you have a number. You have to start somewhere.

While you were trying to recall all of your scenes, you probably started with the most memorable ones: the memorable action, the memorable image, the memorable snippets of dialogue.

Scenes are often remembered through their events, because this is where they come alive. They are the parts of the story where you didn't "have to be there."

But along with remembering each scene comes a feeling charge, on a scale from subtle to extreme. We often don't pay attention to such things, but how you feel about a particular scene contains a great deal of information, and capturing that information is the work of the next two action steps.

## Your "Good" Scenes

I don't think you can go through life writing the same book the whole time. I know people who are growing old doing that. When I say it makes me sad, I don't mean it to sound like a judgment. I just don't want you to have that lack of self-esteem that would keep you from highlighting anything as "good."

"Is it good?" means, "Is it good enough?" Good enough that you don't have to do anything about it right now. Good enough that if you had to show someone one of your scenes, you would be okay with them seeing this one.

You will get to revise all of your scenes later in the method, and when you do you will know so much more about the purpose of a particular scene and the reason for its placement that a few new words will not be hard to find. A good scene probably doesn't need a whole lot more than that.

When you determine that one of the scenes on your list is

good enough, then highlight it in green* and don't look back. About something that I've written, I sometimes think, "It could be better, but I don't know how to make it any better." That's good.

> **Action Step #2: Your Good Scenes**
>
> Highlight the "good" scenes on your list in green, the ones that are done (for now). You are not looking for perfection, which is something different. These are the scenes that "work."

## Your "Bad" Scenes

A bad scene is not morally "bad," obviously; we are assigning *good* and *bad* based on a scene's effectiveness. Sometimes bad scenes are just uninteresting. Sometimes they are unrelated to your theme, and even though you don't have a crystal-clear sense of what your "one thing" is yet, you're pretty sure this isn't it. Sometimes the thought of a bad scene can provoke anxiety—as if its very existence proves that either you are not a good writer or you will not complete this book.

It would be too easy to just jettison a bad scene—after all, you did remember it. As we will see in the next step (which addresses your forgotten scenes), *really* bad scenes are so repetitive

---

* You are highlighting just the scene name, not the entire passage. I've seen people wear their highlighters out that way.

or lifeless that they don't even cross your radar. What we are talking about here is a different kind of bad: scenes that prompt a psychological response ranging from disgruntlement to fear.

A bad scene is like a bad relationship: You have to find out what is bad about it, or else you risk repeating it. With a bad scene, there is something at stake. You're going to learn something, you just haven't learned it yet. You might be afraid to feel something. Maybe you will be able to cut the bad scene loose down the road, if it turns out you are including it only out of duty. But it is also possible to liberate the trapped energy by facing your resistance and turning this "bad" scene into a "good" scene. It may even become one of your favorites, because just when you felt like you were out of options, inspiration arrived.

For now, it's bad. A narrative opportunity was missed here. This scene doesn't do what it was supposed to do. You can't let it out of the house looking like that!

### Action Step #3: Your Bad Scenes

Highlight the "bad" scenes on your list in pink. Your bad scenes are the ones that cause you some anxiety, that nag at you—the ones that you did not nail.

Looking back over your list of scenes, you should now see a lot of "good" and a lot of "bad." You may have some scenes left over about which you don't feel much of anything. Maybe your writing wasn't flowing at the time. You may be tempted to highlight them in some neutral color. But come on, people, this is the big leagues here! If you weren't feeling much of anything, guess what? That's bad!

## Your Forgotten Scenes

In the last step, we identified the "bad" scenes as those that were ineffective or unsettling. I mentioned that the really bad scenes may be the ones you forgot entirely; they may be the scenes that serve no purpose, that advance nothing. In this action step, you will identify your "forgotten" scenes: the ones you were not able to recollect while you were compiling your list.

Why so much emphasis on what you can remember? You may wonder, "What if I forgot to put a great scene on my list? Does that mean I have to get rid of it?" Forgetting a scene doesn't have to be a deal-breaker. The fact that it was forgotten is strike one, not strike three. But it is strike one and should be considered as such.

Every now and then a writer will say, "You know, I've been working on my book for so long, I'm sure I've got every scene memorized." It's never true. Your mind wants to forget certain scenes—it's trying to protect you! If several scenes do the same thing, for example, you will probably remember only one of them. A forgotten scene may be a placeholder for material that you will later develop. Or you may want to use the fact that it was forgotten as evidence to strike it from the book at some point.

Whatever the case, you should have accounted for all of your scenes by the end of this step. As you go through your entire manuscript, you will continue to refine what constitutes a scene in your own style. You may find verbal cues that you have left for yourself as to where a scene begins and ends. This is also a good way to observe how you link scenes together, how you switch from one part of your manuscript to another. My bet is that several of your forgotten scenes were not actually scenes at all, at least not in the sense that we have been working with them; in other words, nothing happened, nothing changed, or the scene was unrelated to the theme of your book.

**Action Step #4: Your Forgotten Scenes**

Go back through your manuscript and identify your "forgotten" scenes. (After this step, your entire manuscript should be divided into scenes.) Give these scenes a name and highlight them in blue, but don't try to assess whether they are "good" or "bad." They are "forgotten."

## Your Missing Scenes

This is not really an action step. As you progress through this method, however, you may be reminded of the scenes that you wanted to write but haven't gotten to yet. Or by poking around and finding holes in the material, you will discover the need for new scenes—a new scene can surprise you at any time. At the very least, give these "missing" scenes a name and add them to your master list; highlight them in orange. If the idea for a new scene comes to you and you want to write it now, please do so!

These missing scenes can show you how your narrative wants to evolve, where the heart of your book truly lies.

## Cut Up Your Scenes

For the final step in this chapter, I am going to urge you to cut up your entire manuscript into its separate scenes. Some writers resist this step; it is scary. You might lose track of the order that the scenes were supposed to go in. Some of your awkward scenes might be exposed, having to stand alone for the first time. You might even lose a scene!

Subconsciously, the belief that your manuscript is Humpty Dumpty may persist: Once broken apart it can never be put back together again. Yet intelligent planning is not the enemy of

Wendy's scenes, cut up with their names on top.

creative genius! On the contrary, such a bold move actually promotes connections between scenes. The scene is now discrete and can eventually be put anywhere in relation to your other scenes. With this flexibility, it is easier to perceive "missing" scenes; a "good" scene might stand nearly alone or be in need of company. With this mobility, it is easier to combine three "forgotten" scenes into one that will actually be "good."

During this step, do not throw anything out or try to microevaluate the elements of an individual scene. While you can separate your scenes into individual files digitally, I prefer the method of physically cutting one scene apart from another and using a stapler to make sure any half pages don't get lost at the beginning or the end of a scene. I think the satisfaction of slicing your manuscript into purposeful ribbons and finishing each pile off with further instructions on a Post-it note is somehow superior to pointing and clicking.

Whichever procedure you choose, cutting up your scenes may make you feel nervous. You will lose track of what scene preceded another so beautifully; you will find chapter titles and numbers tumbling to the wayside. Those chapters you worked so hard to construct are now in rubble, with their building blocks dispersed. You may feel as if you have passed the point of no return. That's not necessarily a bad thing. As I mentioned in the introduction, chances are you have arrived at your revision after some time spent tinkering with your book, as opposed to tackling it. You're going to have to make a break from what you have already created. You may as well make it now, and make it sure, so that you can actually benefit from your revision.

**Action Step #5: Cut Up Your Scenes**

Cut up all of your scenes, either by placing them into individual electronic files or by using scissors and a stapler. This is a radical act that will free your future revision from being a mere derivation of your current draft.

Later in the method, you will get to review your forgotten scenes to see what salvageable material they hold. Likewise, there will come a day of reckoning for those bad scenes that you still can't solve. Your goal then will be to move all of the forgotten, bad, or missing scenes into the category of "good scenes." In Chapter One, I said, "If you find your scenes and put them in the right

Sondra's scenes at the end of the entire method, arranged in a new order and ready for her next draft.

order, you will be all set." I would like to amend that statement slightly. What I meant was, "If you put all your good scenes in the right order, you will be all set."

As with a deck of cards, you will eventually be able to play solitaire with your scenes, picking them up in a certain order as if you were grouping them by suit. For now, you're just trying to make sure you're playing with a full deck.

## Scene: A Note on Nonfiction

If you are writing prescriptive nonfiction or an "idea" book, as opposed to a novel or a work of narrative nonfiction such as a memoir, you may need to translate what *scene* means so that it can best apply to your work. In this chapter, the scenes are marked by those sections that appear below a head or subhead; thus we have eight scenes: *Intro–Good–Bad–Forgotten–Missing–Cut Up–Nonfiction Note.* A scene in nonfiction is a concept, a chunk of necessary information that moves the reader forward. Through the agency of series, you will get the opportunity to build on that concept, to develop it through repetition and variation, and the reader's understanding will grow as he or she is exposed to it in different contexts. A scene in nonfiction can contain diagrams, statistics, quotes from experts, footnotes, and anecdotes; these are all ways that this book, for example, has chosen to obey the dictum "Show, don't tell." Organizing your information if you are writing nonfiction is not that different from when you are writing fiction—what does your reader need to know in what order?

# Series,
# Part I

# Chapter Three

## Series in "The Ugly Duckling"

Our ascent up the mountain of the Book Architecture Method brings us next to *series*. A series is the repetition of a narrative element (such as a person, an object, a phrase, or a place) in such a way that it undergoes a clear evolution. These repetitions—with their attendant variations—may exist in different scenes, or they may exist in the same scene, or both. Over the course of a book-length manuscript, the repetition and variation of narrative elements is what produces meaning.

Series may seem like a complicated concept. I promise that it will be worth it. As David said in class, "Listing our scenes . . . was nice. Separating our scenes helped me get an intuitive read on what needed to be cut and on what I still had to write. But series—that's where it all starts to come together!"

A few details before we get started. In the Book Architecture Method, each item in a series is referred to as an *iteration*. I could have used *occurrence*, or *example*, but I like *iteration* because of its relationship to the word *reiterate*. To reiterate something is to repeat it, any number of times, for emphasis. Nothing is ever the same the second time, however; even if the iteration is repeated exactly, the context has changed. Instead, repetition gives birth to variation—and the interplay between repetition and variation forms the core of the concept of series.

Each time we chart a series, we give it a name (such as IDEN-TITY), and affix an exponent to each iteration to show where it is in the series (e.g., $IDENTITY^1$, $IDENTITY^2$, and so forth). There has been some discussion whether *exponent* is the right term for this superscript number; it is. Iterations of a series literally multiply each other exponentially, which is why they are so powerful and so tricky at the same time.

Oh, and the plural of *series* is *series*. Sorry about that.

## The Weather Series

The best way to convey the operation of series is to see it in action. In the next chapter I will introduce the work of clients and students to help illustrate certain points, but in this chapter we will stick with "The Ugly Duckling" for a bit longer. We will look at four major series, beginning as conversations often do, with the WEATHER. The first two iterations of WEATHER set the scene, reflecting the innocence that accompanies new-born animals. In addition to the name of the series and an expo-nent, I have also noted the scene in which each iteration occurs.

(A completely annotated version of "The Ugly Duckling" with each iteration indicated appears on page 181.)

WEATHER[1]: The country was very lovely just then—it was summer.

*(scene one)*

WEATHER[2]: Next day was gloriously fine, and the sun shone on all the great dock leaves.

*(scene two)*

You may believe that influencing the reader with such effects is manipulative—especially when the weather worsens along with the duckling's fate. Yet it is exactly these parallels that enrich the texture of a narrative; it is similar to the physiological effect of an evocative musical score in a film. In the case of "The Ugly Duckling," we cannot help but experience the downturn in events and what is called a process of deterioration when we encounter the next iterations of the WEATHER series.

WEATHER[3]: The wind whistled so fiercely around the duckling that he had to sit on his tail to resist it, and it blew harder and ever harder.

*(scene four)*

WEATHER[4]: Now autumn came. The leaves in the woods turned yellow and brown. The wind took hold of them, and they danced about. The sky looked very cold and the clouds hung heavy with snow and hail. A raven stood on the fence and croaked, "Caw! caw!" from sheer cold. It made one shiver to think of it.

*(scene five)*

You are probably champing at the bit to identify your own series and may even have begun a list on the sly. We will identify your series in the next chapter, and they don't all have to be one word long, either. One initial stumbling block can be, "How many series should I chart?" This is a variation of the question, "How many scenes should I have?" Since this is a method not a formula, I don't know. But just as I threw out ninety-nine scenes, I'll say twelve to fifteen series for a book-length work. It may help to think of them as your "major" series; those will be the only ones we will be tracking. The temptation to identify everything that repeats and varies in your narrative may be strong, but a series worth keeping track of needs to enter the action at some point—which WEATHER does in the next iteration, influencing the events that befall the main character.

WEATHER[5]: The winter was so bitterly cold that the duckling was obliged to swim about in the water to keep it from freezing over, but every night the hole in which he swam got smaller and smaller . . . At last he was so weary that he could move no more, and he was frozen fast in the ice.

*(scene five)*

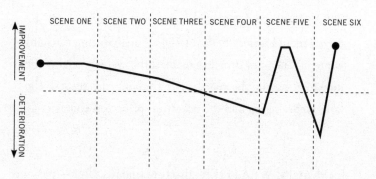

The WEATHER series in "The Ugly Duckling."

In a series that is working, iterations are presented in an order that communicates direction. This evolution may be a "process of deterioration," as we saw in the WEATHER series, or a "process of improvement." Combining deterioration and improvement—the ups and downs, in other words—into an overall movement is what is known as the *narrative arc*. We will create these narrative arcs for your series after we have named them and gotten familiar with them. Constructing an arc is much easier to accomplish when the individual iterations of a series are charted. Above is a graphic representation of the narrative arc of the WEATHER series, charted from scenes one to six on the *x*-axis, and along its relative state of improvement/ deterioration on the *y*-axis.

Examining the next iteration of the series, WEATHER[6], we can see how weather is used to drive the narrative engine, once the series has been established as important in the reader's mind. As the weather worsens, so do our main character's prospects; conversely, a break in the weather alerts us to a change in the duckling's fate.

WEATHER[6]: But it would be too sad to mention all the privation and misery he had to go through during the hard winter. When the sun began to shine warmly again, the duckling was in the marsh, lying among the rushes. The larks were singing and the beautiful spring had come.

*(scene five)*

Incidentally, WEATHER[6] also functions as a link—passages that connect scenes, often in a smooth and unobtrusive manner. By the end of this linking passage, the process of improvement, the upswing, has begun, moving us in the direction of the happy ending that will follow.

## The Ugliness Series

We have observed that series are created by repetition and variation. In the WEATHER series, we saw a familiar narrative element (the weather) repeating in evocative and meaningful iterations. When we look closely at the interplay of repetition and variation in this series, we see some of the advanced effects it creates. For example, in scene five of "The Ugly Duckling," we have three iterations of the WEATHER series; things are getting worse and worse in (what we process as) a relatively short period of time. The pressure that builds up, that desire for a "break in the weather," is something we can see in the next series, UGLINESS, as well.

The first iteration of the UGLINESS series is presented right away in the title: UGLINESS[1]: "The Ugly Duckling." Initially, this series is presented as neutral, but it takes an immediate turn toward deterioration in the very next iteration, remaining there through the first third of the story.

UGLINESS$^2$: How big and ugly he was!

*(scene one)*

UGLINESS$^3$: Even the big ugly gray one swam about with them.

*(scene two)*

UGLINESS$^4$: . . . the other ducks round about looked at them and said, quite loud, "Just look there! Now we are to have that tribe, just as if there were not enough of us already. And, oh dear, how ugly that duckling is! We won't stand him."

*(scene two)*

UGLINESS$^5$: But the poor duckling who had been the last to come out of the shell, and who was so ugly, was bitten, pushed about, and made fun of.

*(scene two)*

UGLINESS$^6$: He was in despair because he was so ugly and the butt of the whole duckyard.

*(scene two)*

UGLINESS$^7$: They were always saying, "If only the cat would get hold of you, you hideous object!"

*(scene three)*

The relentlessness of the UGLINESS series comes from a lack of variation, what amounts to a blunt, obvious repetition. Even the word itself, "ugly," is repeated over and over again, only slightly varied by the use of "monstrous" or "hideous." The fact of the duckling's (alleged) ugliness is established through repetition, and the context of each repetition connects it to his unfortunate plight. This accounts for the comic relief we experience later in scene three, when the wild ducks arrive.

> UGLINESS[8]: "You are so frightfully ugly," said the wild ducks, "but that does not matter to us, so long as you do not marry into our family."
>
> *(scene three)*

> UGLINESS[9]: "I say, comrade," they said, "you are so ugly that we have taken quite a fancy to you!"
>
> *(scene three)*

The idea that ugliness might actually lead to happiness is short-lived, as a hunting party takes out both wild ducks later in the same paragraph. Still, the process of improvement in the UGLINESS series continues, and it contributes to the mystery of the ugly duckling's identity:

> UGLINESS[10]: "Oh, thank Heaven!" sighed the duckling. "I am so ugly that even the dog won't bite me!"
>
> *(scene three)*

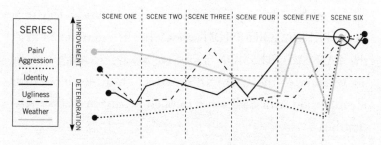

The four major series in "The Ugly Duckling."

## Series Don't Exist in a Vacuum

At this point, you are no doubt becoming aware that series do not exist alone. The UGLINESS series leads to the IDENTITY series; since UGLINESS (beauty) exists in the eye of the beholder, it is in fact inextricably linked to IDENTITY. I always recommend charting our individual series first; when we tease out our series, like separate strands in a piece of cloth, it becomes immensely easier to see what we want to do with each one. It also becomes easier to locate those scenes where two or more series interact. Throughout "The Ugly Duckling" there are several places where series interact, or, to continue the weaving metaphor, where they intertwine. Our word *text* comes from the Latin word *texere*, meaning "woven." For the Romans, a text literally meant the piece of fabric they were writing on, papyrus formed by interwoven reeds. It also gave rise to such words as *context* (what we're talking about here on this piece of papyrus) and *texture*, which is a great word to describe the effect of layering various series on top of each other.

To explore this concept of texture more closely, let's turn to the PAIN/AGGRESSION series.* The first four iterations of the PAIN/AGGRESSION series are always accompanied by an iteration of the UGLINESS series, which enhances their identification with each other through a cause-and-effect relationship.

## The Pain/Aggression Series

If you look at the annotated copy of "The Ugly Duckling," you can see this yoking of the UGLINESS series and the PAIN/AGGRESSION series especially clearly. These series interact in the same paragraph, in subsequent sentences, and even in the same sentence. We may be explicitly told of their connection ("the poor duckling ... who was so ugly, was bitten, pushed about . . ."), but the coexistence of series forges this connection at a subconscious level.

> UGLINESS[2] and PAIN/AGGRESSION[1]: How big and ugly he was! The duck looked at him. "That is a monstrous big duckling," she said. "None of the others looked like that. Can he be a turkey chick? Well, we shall soon find that out. Into the water he shall go, if I have to kick him in myself."
>
> *(scene one)*

* I used to happily call this the PAIN series. Then one student—Dennis, a lawyer who was used to starting only battles he could win—suggested that since the ugly duckling's pain is always inflicted by an enemy, it really should be called the PAIN/AGGRESSION series. I'm convinced.

UGLINESS[4] and PAIN/AGGRESSION[2]: ". . . Now we are to have that tribe, just as if there were not enough of us already. And, oh dear, how ugly that duckling is! We won't stand him." And a duck flew at him at once and bit him in the neck.

*(scene two)*

UGLINESS[5] and PAIN/AGGRESSION[3]: But the poor duckling who had been the last to come out of the shell, and who was so ugly, was bitten, pushed about, and made fun of.

*(scene two)*

UGLINESS[7] and PAIN/AGGRESSION[4]: They were always saying, "If only the cat would get hold of you, you hideous object!" Even his mother said, "I wish to goodness you were miles away." The ducks bit him, the hens pecked him, and the girl who fed them kicked him aside.

*(scene three)*

In these four iterations of the PAIN/AGGRESSION series, nothing of importance actually changes. This is another example of how repetition without variation builds the internal pressure of the story, leading the reader to seek some narrative resolution. The relentlessness of the presentation—and the series being constantly conjoined—leads us to the inevitable conclusion that the duckling's UGLINESS is permanent and that PAIN or AGGRESSION is the natural result of his condition.

Once the repetitions have been clearly established in this way, of course, the variation will have an even more powerful impact on the reader. Consider this brilliant variation of the PAIN/AGGRESSION series:

PAIN/AGGRESSION[5]: Early in the morning a peasant came along and saw him . . . and carried the duckling home to his wife. There he soon revived. The children wanted to play with him, but the duckling thought they were going to ill-use him, and rushed in his fright into the milk pan, and the milk spurted out all over the room.

*(scene five)*

This is just like life; the ugly duckling has seen this scenario unfold one too many times. Having internalized his own sense of ugliness, he now assumes that every creature he meets will want to attack him for it. My wife, who is a psychologist, would say that the ugly duckling had posttraumatic stress disorder, including the characteristics of "persistent re-experiencing of the traumatic event" and "avoidance of stimuli associated with the trauma." The important thing for us to consider here is the twist in this series. Andersen knew what all good storytellers know—that each time an iteration is presented, there is an opportunity to evolve the series to which it belongs.

When we look more closely at the terms *repetition* and *variation*, we can see that we are walking a fine line here. *Repetition* comes from the same root as *repetitive*, and repetitive can get dangerously close to boring. You have to be careful when you have the same event or adjective or discussion happening over and over again.

Recalling our first two definitions of scene, repetition occurs when something happens, and variation occurs when something changes. It stands to reason, then, that you can't have all variation, either. You can't have all change. Yes, variations show skill. Yes, you should be on the lookout for things that can vary, and yes, if you can vary them, you probably should. But it is the pattern created by repetition and variation that communicates meaning. Playing with this pattern can enhance meaning, but bear in mind that your readers are going to search for the pattern first—so help them out.

## The Identity Series

The fourth and final series that we will examine from "The Ugly Duckling" is IDENTITY, which is a prime example of *withholding information*. You may have heard the term *withholding information* in writing circles, or some of its corollaries: "giving readers an IV drip of information, just enough to keep them going," or, "dropping the bread crumbs to lead readers where you want them to go."* But what does withholding information really mean?

---

* I take it this last one is a reference to the fairy tale "Hansel and Gretel"— we'll break that one down next time!

The next chapter will discuss the intricacies, but for now we can say that when you are withholding information, it is necessary to give clues in a subtle or offhand manner without everything "adding up." The first iteration of the IDENTITY series is the title. (This animal is a duckling.) In the second iteration, we see a mother sitting on her nest expecting "her little ducklings." It isn't until the third iteration that we get our first hint of doubt:

> IDENTITY[3]: "This one egg is taking such a long time!" answered the sitting duck. "The shell will not crack . . ."
> "Let me look at the egg which won't crack," said the old duck. "You may be sure that it is a turkey's egg."
>
> *(scene one)*

The doubt continues. The ugly duckling can swim, which means he is not a turkey. Watching him in the water, his mother says:

> IDENTITY[4]: "No, that is no turkey . . . See how beautifully he uses his legs and how erect he holds himself. He is my own chick after all . . ."
>
> *(scene two)*

He may be the best swimmer in the bunch, but by itself, that doesn't prove anything. This is becoming a mystery—we know that we don't know the answer. The duckling is asked, "What sort of a creature are you?" (IDENTITY[5]) and doesn't give a suitable response. Continued confusion about the ugly duckling's identity is wonderfully illustrated in scene four:

> IDENTITY[6]: "What on earth is that?" said the old woman, looking round, but her sight was not good and she thought the duckling was a fat duck which had escaped.
>
> *(scene four)*

If she could see, the argument runs, then would the ugly duckling not be a duckling? Again, nothing is revealed. In scene five, the narrator drops a clue when he tells us that the ugly duckling is viewing "beautiful large birds . . . dazzlingly white with long waving necks." The duckling remains ignorant of their identity (we know them to be swans)—and, by implication, ignorant of its own identity.

The next iteration of the IDENTITY series reads:

> UGLINESS[12] and IDENTITY[8]: He did not know what the birds were, or whither they flew, but all the same he was more drawn towards them than he had ever been by any creatures before. He did not envy them in the least. How could it occur to him even to wish to be such a marvel of beauty? He would have been thankful if only the ducks would have tolerated him among them—the poor ugly creature.
>
> *(scene five)*

With a hint of the PAIN/AGGRESSION series (in the word *tolerate*), this passage almost brings together all of the series we have been studying. This isn't as hard as it first appears. In future action steps we will figure out your individual series and time the iterations of those series in a delightfully logical order. In order to enjoy the full magic of series, we first need to examine the scenes where our series interact. I call those your *key scenes*, and they are the focus of the next chapter.

# Chapter Four

# Key Scenes and Your Series

In the previous chapter, we charted four different series in "The Ugly Duckling" and made two basic observations. First, when series are isolated, it is much easier to examine their development and their impact; second, series don't exist in a vacuum. Series will always intersect, and when they do, they interact; they inform one another. These occasions, when series come together in a proximate, physical, literal sense, give a reader the feeling that "it is all coming together." Scenes in which two or more series intersect are called *key scenes*.

When series interact, anything can happen. They can conflict and send one another spinning. One series can slow another down or stop it all together. One series can end within another, which will become important later when we discuss the obstacles or fresh complications that a narrative needs to remain compelling. All of these are options, provided that you have key scenes. If you don't have key scenes, if your series don't intersect that often, you may have found the root of the problem with your manuscript. This often comes about in the middle of a narrative, where the length of time a reader has invested in your work is not being repaid—the payoff lies in being able to make the connections that key scenes produce when series intersect. But my bet is that you do have some key scenes, at least enough for us to get started.

## The Key Scene in "The Ugly Duckling"

Key scenes makes it easier to find our series, which is why we start there. But how do we know we have a key scene, and how does it differ from a good scene? A key scene needs to be good (as do all of the other scenes in your book eventually)—but not all good scenes are key scenes. A good scene may be an important scene, a memorable scene, but it is not necessarily a key scene unless it contains the maximum interaction of series. Let's look at "The Ugly Duckling" and try to determine which is the key scene. (In short stories, it's a little easier—that's the only hint I'm going to give you!)

Sometimes students identify the key scene in "The Ugly Duckling" as scene two. They find the characters endearing and the descriptions evocative; dramatic tensions are building, which draw them in emotionally. Scene two is a good scene, but it is not a key scene. Since a key scene is where a maximum number of series interact, it is rarely located in the first third of the text—the individual series have simply not had time yet to be sufficiently established.

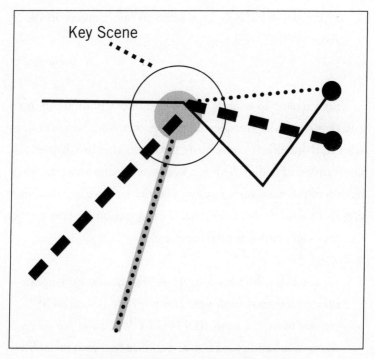

Key Scene

A key scene is where series come together.

In "The Ugly Duckling" the key scene is scene six, the last scene. In what basically amounts to a suicide attempt (fairy tales have gotten so soft nowadays!), every series we have identified interacts:

> "I will fly to them, the royal birds (IDENTITY[9]), and they will hack me to pieces (PAIN/AGGRESSION[6]) because I, who am so ugly (UGLINESS[13]), venture to approach them. But it won't matter! Better be killed by them than be snapped at by the ducks, pecked by the hens, spurned by the henwife

(PAIN/AGGRESSION[6]), or suffer so much misery in the
winter (WEATHER[8])."

*(scene six)*

It is amazing to witness, really. The interactions are so intri-
cate that they raise the question of whether Andersen set out to
achieve these effects consciously (more on this in Chapter Six;
short answer: He did). This is a key scene because it is the intersection of the maximum number of series we have been examining. At the end of this key scene, the interaction of series creates
the emotional payoff for the reader.

> He saw below him his own image, but he was no longer a
> clumsy dark gray bird, ugly and ungainly (UGLINESS[14]).
> He was himself a swan (IDENTITY[10])! . . . The big swans
> swam round and round him and stroked him with their bills
> (PAIN/AGGRESSION[7]).

*(scene six)*

One reason this scene has such an impact is that all four series are together in one place. In addition, the repetition and
variation have been handled with skill; many iterations are the
opposite of what we have come to expect. Our protagonist is not
UGLY and ungainly; beauty greets him instead in his reflection.
Instead of continually being at a loss, his IDENTITY is revealed
as something he can be proud of. This reversal of fortune—this
process of deterioration becoming a process of improvement—is
especially intense in the PAIN/AGGRESSION series where, instead of abuse, the ugly duckling (now a young swan) receives

attention and nurture, signified of course by the wonderful WEATHER.

---

**Action Step #6: Your Key Scenes**

Go through your list of scenes and identify your "key" scenes by placing an asterisk next to their name. You can add to this list later, as you expand your series; the point now is just to get started.

---

"How do I know for sure which are my key scenes?" you may be wondering by now. Remember: method, not formula. You are completing these action steps to more closely examine the workings of your manuscript at this point. You do not have to get these exercises "right." Nevertheless, here are some general guidelines to keep in mind as you try to identify your key scenes:

- A key scene does not usually exist in the first third of your narrative. (Think scene six in "The Ugly Duckling," not scene two.) Key scenes require other scenes to lay the groundwork for their impact.

- Don't worry about finding scenes where a "maximum number of series" interact—that's for later. For now, look for scenes where two (or more) series interact.

- You can have more than one key scene, of course, especially if you are writing a book-length work. You may have ninety-nine scenes and eleven key scenes where at least two series intersect.

- Unlike our example from "The Ugly Duckling," in a book-length work, the key scene is rarely last. We need time after a key scene, in the form of additional scenes, to understand the ramifications.

- A key scene may be near the top of the list of scenes you brainstormed originally, as these scenes are typically very memorable.

- A key scene contains an emotional payoff. Or conversely, as Stacey observed, it is the "least likely to be nuanced." (Stacey was writing a novel about Joe from Cleveland, so she understood lack of nuance.)

- A key scene is a point of no return, marked by profound changes or the occurrence of major consequences.

## Naming Your Series

Once you have identified your key scenes, you can detect the major movements that exist within them; these are your series. Start a list, naming each series as you named each scene: with something you can remember that will bring you quickly back into the essence of that series. What constitutes a series? A person, a place, or a thing is a good place to start. Anything that repeats and varies should be considered, specifically real things. Series can be conceptual, but you have to be careful—an abstract series such as "DEATH" or "DISCOVERY" may include too many things and be difficult to track through all of its iterations. In Linda's memoir, "CANCER" was a series because it helped us track the main character's improvement vs. deterioration, but so was "JEWELRY"—to forge her own identity, Linda chooses not to work in her father's jewelry business; she gets a ring with no fanfare from the wrong guy; her mother dies of cancer and Linda comes into possession of her diamond that only needs to be reset; and finally a proper proposal (with reset ring!) comes in Tuscany from the right guy.

Remember the following when you name your series:

- A series is where things repeat; by definition there needs to be more than one iteration in a series.

- A series is where things vary. So a series might be found where something changes—it might be a character as he or she evolves, a relationship that has its ups and downs, or an object that becomes a symbol.

- A series needs a name. It doesn't have to be one word long, but it should be short enough to handle easily. The name should bring you back into the essence of what the series is about.

- You are shooting for twelve to fifteen series.

- Don't make your series about too big a concept! That is the most common mistake I see made at this action step.*

- Series can often be found intersecting with other series (and eventually will have to do so to earn their place in the final draft). Something is triggered by something else that was to that point unrelated.

---

**Action Step #7: Name Your Series**

Begin a list of your series by identifying the major movements that exist within your key scenes. Name each series just as you named each scene: with something you can remember that will bring you quickly back into the essence of that series.

---

Ed was writing a book called *8 Habits of Love*. Each habit was a practice that one could engage in—compassion, generosity, and so on—that would transport us as individuals from a state of fear into a state of love. That was his theme, what in nonfiction might also be considered a *premise*. As I mentioned earlier, twelve to fifteen series is a manageable number of series

---

* In writing this book, for example, I gave up tracking the MOST COMMONLY HEARD EXPRESSIONS IN WRITING CIRCLES and focused on tracking SHOW, DON'T TELL instead. A series has to be small enough to register for the reader.

to track for a book-length work.* To come up with Ed's list, we focused on the series that interacted with other series, that had an impact on the narrative as a whole, and that helped to shape or convey meaning:

1. *Hope*, Ed's wife. She was an important part not only of his present spiritual life but of his "spiritual autobiography."
2. *Thomas Merton*, a Franciscan monk who was Ed's intellectual mentor, whose writing illuminated the development of Ed's thinking at critical junctures.
3. *Rabbi Friedman*, a real-life mentor who brought Ed in and eventually gave him his blessing and sent him on his way.

We considered the preceding his three "character" series. (If you were wondering whether characters can be an example of series, they can! We will explore this later in the chapter.) His "idea" series were more numerous, because of the kind of book he was writing:

4. *The Habits Themselves.* Each habit was the focus of its own chapter (e.g., "The Habit of Stillness") and

---

* If that seems like a lot, remember that you are actually tracking dozens of series all the time: what certain characters in a novel like to eat, what time of day it is, what the last thing somebody said to somebody was. It is important to keep all of these minor details straight, especially if your work has gone through multiple revisions, but you don't have to track a hundred series.

repeated with variations throughout the chapter
that bore its name. The foundational habits also
recurred in later chapters (e.g., "Stillness" in
"Candor,") so those iterations had to be tracked.

5. *How-to*, or "the takeaway." Each chapter contained
   specific suggestions for how to practice each habit,
   going into some detail (e.g., "The Habit of Stillness"
   discussed sitting, breathing, focusing, etc.).

6. *Love and Fear*. Ed had a series in which these two
   paramount concepts were imagined in a spatial
   relationship: Through the practice of any given
   habit, one moved from the house of fear into the
   house of love.

7. *The Philosophy of Nonviolence*. Not in every chapter
   (we don't want to get too predictable—even in
   nonfiction!) but in many there were iterations of
   the philosophy of nonviolence, such as Ed's status
   as a conscientious objector during Vietnam and
   Archbishop Tutu's post-apartheid gentle reckoning
   with pathological criminals.

Because nonfiction benefits just as much from the use of
scene as fiction does—albeit with slightly different qualifica-
tions for what constitutes a scene—Ed had several "scenic" series, of which I will only mention two:

8. *All Saints Church*. All Saints was the Episcopalian
   church where Ed was the rector, where he gave a
   number of his most influential sermons, and where

a number of the "counseling conversations"
contained in his book took place.

9. *Parishioner Stories.* Like the student and client
examples in this book (I hope!), anecdotes involving
the men and women who made up Ed's congregation
made the grander concept of "Habits of Love" more
accessible because they were more human.

I have detailed nine of Ed's series here for the sake of example; by the end of his book-length work (250 to 400 pages) we
were tracking more like eighteen series. How many series you
track depends in part on how long your work is. In "The Ugly
Duckling," we have tracked four. If we really tried, we could
probably find twenty series in "The Ugly Duckling." There could
be a BEAUTY series (very pretty ducklings, handsome children), which would help reveal the UGLINESS series. There
could be a ROOTLESSNESS series (you don't have to go home,
but you can't stay here). There could be a BIRD series (duckling,
swan, turkey, stork, wild goose, hen, lark) that conflicts with a
NONBIRD series (cat, hunting dog, human).

Jenny found that she had twenty-nine series—and her manuscript was only a little over a hundred pages! Her scenes could
not bear the weight of this many series carrying meaning through
their repetitions and variations. The reader was left feeling over-
whelmed, unable to keep track of so many ideas that didn't have
time to sink in. By going through each of her series carefully, she
was able to craft a shorter list; she found some series that could
be combined and some series that could be safely eliminated because they had only one or two minor iterations.

## Action Step #8: Expand Your List of Series

Review the rest of your manuscript to expand your list of series until you have twelve to fifteen of them. Pay special attention to your "good scenes" for clues. Identify each iteration of a series by giving it an exponent.

This is usually when people start saying, "This is a lot of work!" My usual response is, "Either way, it's going to be a lot

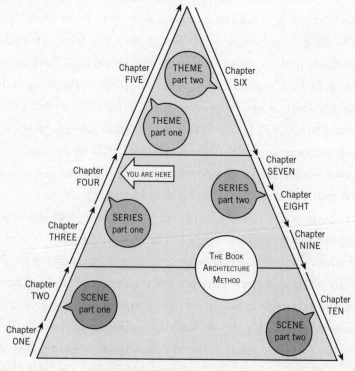

The Book Architecture Method,
some serious climbing behind us.

of work." At least with this method, you can be confident that you are working toward something substantially stronger than your current draft. Besides, the thrill of making it to the top of our metaphorical mountain, where you will be able to discover what your book is really about, will make the journey well worth your effort.

## The Implications of Series

How you handle your series will determine your readers' forward progress and their level of commitment to your work. Series is how people become characters, how objects become symbols, and how a message repeated becomes the moral of your story. Now that you have engaged in greater depth with your own series, I would like to explain why I don't use the word *plot* in this book. For one thing, it is a term with nearly unlimited associations. It's hard to get anybody to focus on what is actually going on in their book while they are worried about whether their plot is good. For another thing, *plot* is singular, as if it somehow references everything. As such, you can't work with a plot.

Working on the level of individual series, however—charting each series as it undergoes a recognizable process of improvement or deterioration—is possible. And beyond that, it is necessary—especially if you want to create a rich experience for the reader, one that is satisfying yet unexpected. A complex book does not come from complex series that are difficult to navigate; that's called confusion. Complexity comes from clear, meaningful series that intersect and interact in unusual and consequential ways.

This isn't quite as hard as it looks. In this book, for example, you have grown accustomed to the NINETY-NINE SCENES series, the HIGHLIGHTER COLOR series (for good scenes, bad scenes, etc.), the DEFINITIONS OF SCENE series (of which we have three out of a promised five), and many more. Once we take a methodical look at our work, it will yield; we will be able to tease apart the various strands from our textile/text.

Having isolated individual series as well as noting the occasions where they intersect, we are in a better position to reflect on some of the implications of series—continuing the realization that we may know more about this subject than we thought. Consider terms such as *suspense, surprise,* and *shock.* Suspense, surprise, and shock are all ways an author withholds information; in the context of series we can examine how the technique of withholding information really operates.

Suspense, surprise, and shock are created by the relative distance between iterations in a particular series. The effect of suspense is achieved when we are continually told what we don't know. *Will the ugly duckling ever find a place to rest without the threat of getting maimed?* is an example of suspense. (He can't stay in the nest, he can't stay in the old woman's house, and he obviously can't stay frozen in ice.) The iterations are closer together and they are well managed to produce the effect that something is imminently going to be communicated to us.

When the gaps between iterations are longer, surprise occurs. This is true in the IDENTITY series; we know we have a question, but we forget for a while that it is a question. *Just what kind of a creature is this ugly duckling?* is the focus of intense scrutiny in the first three scenes, and then it recedes from our conscious mind for some time until the swans appear at the beginning of scene five. When an individual series suddenly returns to our conscious mind after such a pause and we experience the next iteration as unique yet familiar, this is surprise.

Shock occurs when there is barely one iteration before a disclosure takes place. When the wild ducks are gunned down, we are shocked—but somewhere in the recesses of our mind we knew this was a possibility; the "great dock leaves" under whose shadow the ducklings begin their swimming adventures in fact grow from the walls of a house, an old mansion, hinting at human inhabitants. With shock there needs to be something that would have admitted this possibility—the iteration that delivers a shock seems to come out of nowhere while not being totally unexpected in hindsight.

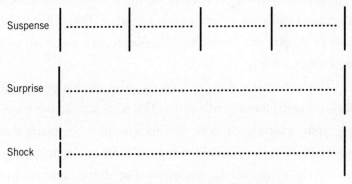

In suspense, there are regular iterations that withhold information; in surprise, the gap between iterations gets longer; in shock, we never truly get the first iteration, only a hint at it.

Managing the gaps between your iterations is important for the flow of your book. When you place an iteration on page 7, for example, another on page 17, and then the culmination of the series on page 297 with nothing in between, most readers will have reassigned the brain cell that was supposed to be remembering the original information. Unless the reader is studying your manuscript for a grade (or for a living), he or she will need this material brought to mind more frequently, or any chance you have at producing revelation will be lost.

How iterations are spaced out is also related to the concept of *foreshadowing*. An iteration that occurs early on in a series, that sets us up for what is to come, performs an important role—not only does it establish the existence of a series in the narrative, but how it is presented (emotional tone, exact situation) helps determine how the series will lodge in a reader's mind. Anton Chekhov often advised budding playwrights that a gun in the first act must go off in the third. What he meant by that is that if a hunting rifle that is hung on a scenic backdrop is the focus of some discussion earlier in a play, it must be pulled down off the wall later in the play and brandished at someone, or even better, used to shoot somebody.

The first act is not so far from the third act that people will forget that the hunting rifle exists. This is critical. To put it simply, your readers need to be able to remember the material in your narrative that you want to have an effect on them. It is okay to introduce a red herring (an iteration or several iterations that are intended to throw readers off the trail), as long as readers can remember it along with what they were really supposed to remember.

This discussion of the role of memory brings me to one final point. When possible, reduce the number of series that you are having the reader track. If something is working, why not see how far it can go instead of switching to another series just to include something else? Use it, don't include it. Or to say it another way: If you're going to include it, use it.

## Series: A Note on Character

One place to begin building out your list of series is to consider each of your major characters as his or her own individual series. (As in Ed's case, if you are writing a nonfiction book, your characters can be either expert voices or otherwise influential people to whom you refer regularly.) Character is the ultimate example of series; the terms *character arc* and *narrative arc* are often used interchangeably in writing circles. Bear in mind that a main character may very well belong to more than one series on your list.

When we explored what happens and what changes in "The Ugly Duckling," we used the terms *repetition* and *variation*. For some reason, writers find it more helpful to use the words *identity* and *change* when they bring their characters into the context of series.

For the most part, these terms mean the same thing. Their relationship is shown in the following analogy:

**repetition : variation :: identity : change**

Writers can associate identity with the static quality of a

character better than repetition, although when you think about it, people do repeat from day to day. It is the way in which they repeat (dialect, costume, outlook, relationships, etc.) that earns a well-drawn character the praise of being "consistent" or the criticism that they have acted "out of character." Knowing what to expect from a character not only makes his or her change more dramatic, it also helps us identify the character in the first place.

How much change a character goes through is of course a matter of personal choice. E. M. Forster distinguished between a *flat character* and a *round character*. A flat character is a minor character whose part is so small that he or she doesn't have time to change, while a round character\* may go through a change of heart so transformative, and the writer may portray it so well, that the reader undergoes a change along with the character, an empathic experience known as *catharsis*.

Catharsis was introduced by Aristotle. He said that through a process of identification, the viewers of a drama (or readers of a book, in our case) could have their emotions purified when they experienced pity and fear through absorbing the events of a story. As the goal of dramatic writing, catharsis has survived. I would argue that we read books because we want to believe that people can change. That is the most thrilling possibility we can imagine. It keeps us engrossed in narrative of all forms, from advertising to religious myth. We want to believe that people can change. We want to believe that *we* can change.

---

\*   To this, Evelyn Waugh objected that all fictional characters were flat; he preferred to cast the distinction this way: "There are the protagonists and there are characters who are furniture. One gives only one aspect of the furniture."

The interesting thing about change is that it often returns us to who we truly were to begin with. This is the premise of, among other models, Joseph Campbell's *Hero with a Thousand Faces*: the protagonist returns home from a journey with the boon of greater awareness. Series allow us to have our cake and eat it too—change allows for a deeper and more solid sense of identity; the variations reinforce the true nature of the repetition. This is why a series promotes the concept of unity better than unity can speak up for itself. And remember, unity is what we are truly after with the series work we have done in this chapter—and will do in the next.

# Theme,
# Part I

# Chapter Five

# Your One Thing

Your book can only be about one thing, which I call your *theme*. Your book can't be about ninety-nine things; those are your scenes. Your book can't be about twelve to fifteen things; those are your series. You might have heard about the *themes* (plural) that a good book has; those are what we are now calling series. You can have only one theme.

I say this so often that one writer said, "Your book can only be about one thing—that's your one thing." This idea probably runs counter to what you have been told about book-length manuscripts requiring complexity, ambiguity, or even sheer volume. How are you supposed to fill up a whole book's worth of pages unless you include everything you can think of?

But that's not how structures work. Think about it. Life might be about war and art and love and coming-of-age friendships and betrayal and exercise and career and spirituality, but life gets 168 hours a week. Readers will give your book 10 hours of their time, on average.

"What about two things?" Sasha asked. Her novel was about love and music. "Can your book be about two things?"

"Yes, it can," I replied. "Provided those two things are about one thing." In Sasha's case, the music arc and the love arc followed each other closely; it was how the main characters met, the cause of passion, jealousy, and confusion between them, and eventually what caused their undoing. Her book was about the music of love; that was her theme.

I'm warning you now: Sometimes a condensed, one-sentence theme may look like a cliché. Bear in mind that the value a theme has for informing this process does not come from its originality. It comes from being about one thing.

Here are some examples of themes from our class:

"I found myself, and my man found me."

"It's not how you fall in life, it's how you pick yourself up."

"Heaven is no place for angels."

Except for the last one perhaps, these are all pretty cliché—yet they generated the necessary cohesion for strong books. Linda (she of the CANCER and JEWELRY series, among others) had a theme that read: *Everything happens for a reason; you just don't get the reason at the same time as the thing.* Call that a cliché if you want; a recognizable theme has to be already in the hearts of your readers somewhere. When we arrived at Linda's theme we were able to tell at a glance which scenes, series, and characters served her book's purpose and which could be safely discarded.

How you go about finding your theme is the focus of this chapter. Discovering your theme can seem like an overwhelming task at first, and it does involve a lot of messy scribbling. We will break the process into three successive steps: a theme in four sentences, in two sentences, and in one sentence. The first of these, the four-sentence variety, is also known as "the elevator pitch."

Your book can only be about one thing, and you have to be able to say what that one thing is. This is not distortion, although it is good marketing. Some people refuse to put an elevator pitch together because they claim it is reductive (um, obviously). Their friends ask them, "Oh, you're writing a book. What's it about?" And they answer, "I don't know. You're just going to have to read it and find out."* Linda didn't have time for that tomfoolery. Now she was able to say, "It's about how everything happens for a reason . . . you just don't get the reason at the same time as the thing." To which her friends and family invariably responded, "Am I in it?"

## Describe Your Series

Do you remember writing down what you thought your book was about back in Chapter One? It seemed like it was going to

---

* These are the same people who drink coffee out of mugs with Picasso's face and his quote printed on the side: "Painting is stronger than I am. It makes me do what it wishes."

be easy to say what your book is about—after all, you're writing it. But it wasn't, really. Most of the time your one thing emerges only after a careful examination of your work. You get a glimpse of your true theme, and eventually a grasp of it. The question is, how do you get there? The answer is, by studying your series.

Assigning descriptive phrases or sentences to your series will help you answer the question, "What is my book about?" If it seems like we are discussing your series and your theme at the same time, we are: We have entered one of those mountain vegetation zones where different flora exist side by side. Your series go to the heart of what happens and what changes in your work; the individual narrative arcs, taken together, form the overall narrative arc that is your theme.

In the next action step you will describe each of your series in a single sentence. As you complete these, it may be helpful for us to do the same exercise for the series we found in "The Ugly Duckling." Remember, a good sentence will capture what happens and what changes in your series. On the other hand, since this is a method, and the point is to keep going, don't agonize over these sentences. (I'm not agonizing over these series sentences from "The Ugly Duckling," believe me.)

UGLINESS: As a young swan grows up he goes from being perceived as the ugliest animal in the duckyard to the most handsome.

PAIN/AGGRESSION: Because of his supposed "ugliness," a young swan is subject to attack to the point where he

internalizes his fear of others and avoids intimacy altogether.

IDENTITY: A supposed "ugly duckling" that fails to fit in
wanders until he discovers his true identity as a young
swan.

WEATHER: The weather gets worse as the "ugly duckling's"
fate worsens, then gets better to herald a new beginning.

---

### Action Step #9: Describe Your Series

Describe each of your series in one sentence that shows
both its identity and the change it undergoes. If a series
does not undergo a change (if there is no appreciable
variation within its repetition), notice that as well!

---

## List Your Series Sentences

After you have written a sentence for every series, the next action
step is to put these sentences in an order of importance. Journal-
ists know this as the *inverted pyramid*, conveyed by the well-
known adage "Don't bury your lead." They are trained to begin
with the most critical detail first (the headline) because they
know at some point people will stop reading. We can learn from
this practice. Just because a series ends up near the bottom in
importance does not mean you have to take it out of your book.
It just means it has less relevance to the task of discovering your
theme.

**Action Step #10: List Your Series Sentences**

List your series sentences in a top-down order of importance.

## Your One Thing

In the next action step we will combine your series sentences from a dozen or more in number to a four-sentence thematic statement first, then to a two-sentence expression, and finally to the one sentence that is your theme. This work is a bit like reducing a marinara sauce under high heat. You don't want to damage any of the ingredients, but you have to end up with less.

When Kimberly combined and eliminated her series sentences in class, this was her first pass:

> In my novel, the main character is forced to give up her illegitimate child and for years she is detached from normal life. She is forced into a work program that changes her view of her own life, as outside influences force her to face her current situation and pick a path moving forward. Her journey is about finding hope, accepting the past, and choosing a future.

Many four-sentence statements (and Kimberly wants me to point out that this is only three) have a lot of who, what, where, when, and why in them. This is good for an elevator pitch, but it needs further reduction for you to arrive at your theme.

Kimberly's two-sentence statement was obtained by eliminating the lines that attempted to sum up and place the action.

> Outside forces force Samantha to face her current situation and pick a path moving forward. Her journey is about finding hope, accepting the past, and choosing a future.

The last line in this version is unchanged and presents what looks like the theme—yet it is still too broad. While the three actions—finding hope, accepting the past, and choosing a future—are obviously related, each could be the theme of a book. They are three things, rather than one thing. Kimberly says that in her notebook, this is what she circled:

> choosing a future

"Choosing a future" is rich enough that it implies other necessary actions; it is internally wound in a way that provokes both curiosity and identification in the reader. "I want to read about that," someone might say. "That might affect me today."

Themes need to be at least two words long: a subject and a verb. "Conformity" isn't enough, for example, while "conformity corrodes" is plenty. "Conformity corrodes" has both a subject that can be limited, or at least bounded, and a verb that might operate through all of the major actions of a book. Having a subject and a verb is akin to having a topic and an angle at the same time.

Of course, themes do not have to be only a few words; they can also be a full sentence. Rich's theme was twenty-eight words. Going through this exercise in class, we found it on page 193:

To the outside world, the Navy may appear to be black and white; to the officers and men that served, the Navy was a thousand shades of gray.

Rich's theme contains both the specificity of a good theme—we know what world the action takes place in—and the twist in the action, the unrest that will generate scenes of interest leading to a conclusion.

Is there really a key that will turn the engine of your book? Chances are, yes. I have worked with writers of all skill levels, published and not (and not yet). Inevitably their theme is present in their work; it seems to be human nature to want to put those one or two sentences into one's book that will explain the whole thing. Finding yours can be an "aha" moment.

> **Action Step #11: Your One Thing**
>
> Distill your many series sentences into four, focusing on the largest series and their interactions. Continue to combine elements until this statement is two sentences, and then only one: This is your theme.

## Message, Moral, and Mantra

Returning to our trusty text, "The Ugly Duckling," we can find the theme expressed in a sentence in the key scene (I told you I wasn't making this up!).

It does not matter in the least having been born in a duckyard, if only you come out of a swan's egg.

*(scene six)*

In stating the theme of his story, Andersen takes a position
that you may or may not agree with. You may feel that his "message" is stated a little baldly, and indeed, that is his style—and
the style in vogue during his time, as well as for fairy tales pretty
much all the time. It is no accident that in fairy tales the theme
is often called "the moral" of the story. While Andersen never
really misses an opportunity to hold forth, many current writers
(who have been steeped in postmodernism) chafe against the
concept of delivering a message. But you do not have to be prescriptive about your reader's actions to be able to articulate your
theme.

Your theme can be *ambiguous* (meaning it takes us in several
possible directions at once). Your theme can be *ambivalent* (meaning it can contain mixed feelings and events, often represented
by different characters). It does not have to be your message or
your moral, but it will turn into your mantra.

Your book can only be about one thing. In the next chapter
we're going to make sure it's something good.

# Theme,
# Part II

# Chapter Six

# The Vista of Revision

So far, this whole book has been about organization more than revision. That's why you have gone on your arduous trek up the mountain. Having just crested the top—with the discovery of your theme, the one thing your book is about—you are now on the way down. But as I said before, you don't want to go down the same way you came up. What fun would that be?

Think about the word *revision* for a minute. Forget about the dictionary; let's just try to define it ourselves. Revision means looking at the same thing again. When we do this, we see that it both is and is not the same thing as it was before. That's why our themes can often come as a surprise and still be deeply rewarding at the same time.

My client Julie was nearly stunned to learn that her book was about "lotus flower living," a metaphor for discovering and holding on to spiritual experience. Yet *Lotus Flower Living* had been her title since we started working together. In a way, she had to earn the right to write about her subject; it's one thing to say you're going to write a book about something and quite another to climb a mountain of material—some good, some bad, some key, some still missing—and realize what you've actually written about.

To continue the metaphor, it is the going that reveals the terrain. How could it be otherwise? If you already knew everything you would see or experience, you wouldn't write a book, climb a mountain, take a trip, or start talking to a stranger in the hopes that you might fall in love. (Okay, maybe the last one of these

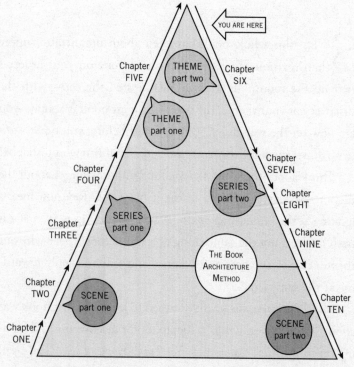

Having crested the top, let yourself take it all in.

isn't such a good idea.) As E. M. Forster said, "How can I know what I think until I see what I say?"*

## Accept Control

From the top, you can see forever. The next action step encourages you to believe two things: you can gain the clarity necessary to revise your work, and you can gain the courage to take your book in any direction that it wants to go. Let's take clarity first. By now I've probably convinced you that one of the most important things about themes is that they emerge. Books written initially with a central theme in mind, a "philosophy," are often pale and awkward, while books written from the need to express one's reality are inventive and energetic.

Hopefully you have discovered your theme, and if you're like most people you will probably have found it sitting right there, waiting only for you to have the eyes to see it. If you're still unsure about your theme, see what your beta readers think your book is about. Instead of telling them what you want to believe your book is about, ask them, "What is the theme of this work? What is the one thing that this book is about?" You might be surprised!

Remember scribbling down your theme back in Chapter One?

---

* There are many sayings in this regard, proving its validity in my mind. Bob Marrs lists, among others, "I think at the typewriter" (Arthur Miller), "To be a writer does not mean to present a truth, it means to *discover* a truth" (Milan Kundera), and "When you're writing, you're trying to find out something which you don't know. The whole language of writing for me is finding out what you don't want to know, what you don't want to find out" (James Baldwin).

You probably kept that in a safe place, as most writers have the sense of an archivist. Go back and look at that theme. Chances are it isn't that much different from what you are working with now. I compare it to a clock with hands that move to one o'clock from twelve o'clock. Your original idea was right, but through all of your writing and subsequent efforts at organization, your theme has evolved, moved forward. Time marches on.

That's the clarity part; embracing a subtly (or not-so-subtly) different perspective on what you are doing is where the courage comes in. We have asked the question, "Is this my theme?" Now we can ask the question, "Do I *want* this to be my theme? Given what I know about my work (and myself), does this reflect my values?" If all lights are green in that direction, then the only question remaining is, "How far can I push it?"

It is possible, if not to change your theme, at least to steer it, to shift it into a fitting expression of what you believe and can deliver on. If you wrote your way in, you can write your way out. After you have felt the import of what you are currently doing, rewrite your four-line thematic statement to gear your efforts even closer to your true intent. What is the one thing you want your revision to be about?

### Action Step #12: Accept Control

Examine your theme closely. Is it reflective of your beliefs? Is it entitled to your precious time and painstaking effort? Is it entitled to your reader's precious time and painstaking effort? How should it be altered to more closely align with the book you want (or need) to write?

## Tyranny of the First Draft

All writers revise. That is the answer to a question I get a lot.

Take Hans Christian Andersen, for example (you knew this was coming). The original title of "The Ugly Duckling" was "The Young Swans." Thank God he changed that, huh? It would have ruined everything, and besides, that first title is just not good!

The change in the title indicates that as Andersen became progressively more aware of what he was writing, he was simultaneously engaged in making important choices regarding how he wanted his story to go.

So do I really think Andersen thought about the kinds of things that the Book Architecture Method teaches, such as scene and series and theme? Do I really think Andersen thought about his craft to the level that we are thinking about his craft, and our own?

I do. What is the alternative? Either we believe Andersen and other famous writers are better writers than we are—they don't need to go through the same processes that we do, because they're just geniuses and stuff . . . or we believe that thinking too hard about what you are doing creatively will ruin it—because that's somehow not Zen, or at least that's not where true inspiration comes from.

To a certain degree, these kinds of thoughts are natural. We are engaged in creating something new. Because it is new, we don't know where it's coming from, by virtue of its not having been here before. We may get very mystical about the writing rituals that have helped us achieve solid writing—I know I do. But that's different from believing that every word that came to us the first time is qualitatively better than any word that will come to us the next time. We persist in believing that certain elements in our document now can't be rearranged or eliminated.

I call this *the tyranny of the first draft*. It might just as well be called *the tyranny of the previous draft*, because any draft that is done, that has been sent to an editor or is sitting in the printer, is somehow more authoritative than what we will produce in the future. But judging from the past fruits of our creative process, this feeling is only an illusion. Everything changes. It's the courage to help our material evolve that we need to summon, so that we can actually improve matters, as opposed to simply stagnate.

## Draw the Target

Now that you have your theme securely in hand, it is time to see how close to the mark your current material is, to examine more closely the degree to which your scenes and series are being employed in service to your theme. The next action step invites you to draw an archery-like target and place your theme at the center, in the bull's-eye. There is no preferred media for this: digitally works, for those of us who are technologically advanced, but so do Post-it notes on a larger piece of poster board, or tagged pins attached to a piece of fabric.

Or you can just draw it, as the step suggests! We drew Rich's in class on a blackboard. Remember Rich? His twenty-eight-word theme was waiting for him on page 193 of his work in progress.

To the outside world, the Navy may appear to be black and white; to the officers and men that served, the Navy was a thousand shades of gray.

We put "1,000 Shades of Gray" at the center of the target and invited fellow students to suggest elements of Rich's book: It could be a scene, a series, a character, a place, or an event—anything, so long as everyone knew what we were referring to.

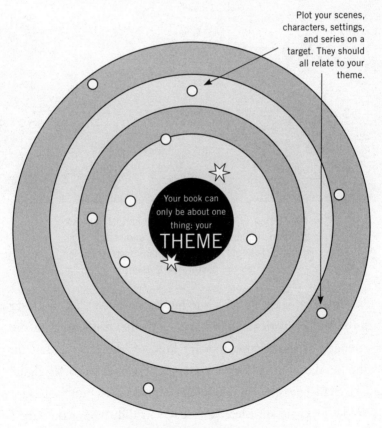

Plot your scenes, characters, settings, and series on a target. They should all relate to your theme.

Your book can only be about one thing: your THEME

Your book can only be about one thing—now as a visual!

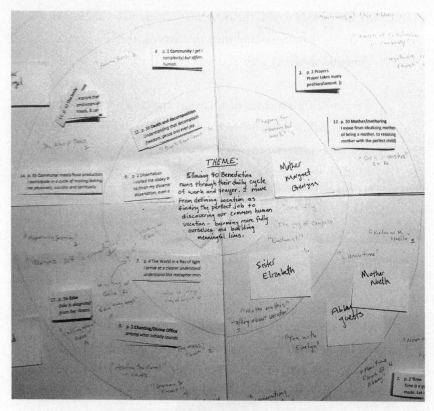

Jenny's target with her theme in the middle, series on folded and stapled pieces of paper, and characters on yellow Post-it notes. Her scene names are scribbled on the poster board itself.

The trick of the exercise is to put the narrative element closer to or farther from the bull's-eye, or theme, depending on the strength of the relationship. It's kind of like Pin the Tail on the Donkey, but your eyes are open. It should be easier, right? The challenge is, of course, as I encouraged in Action Step Zero: "How to Generate Material," that you didn't have the target when you started writing. Instead it's like you threw a bunch of darts against a bare wall, and now you are trying to draw the target around where most of the darts landed.

In Rich's case, as a first-time novelist writing loosely from his personal experiences, he had too many scenes and characters. The point of this exercise was to help him define which of those added consistency and coherence to the story and which should be deleted: Would the manipulative yet persuasive U.S. senators go closer to or further from the "1,000 Shades of Gray" theme? Closer. How about the scene where a Russian submarine captain refuses to sink a U.S. boat because the kinship he feels to those fellow submariners who brave the ocean's brutality outweighs the contrived differences of the cold war? Definitely closer.

What about the scenes of sailors participating in risqué activities such as drinking, gambling, and womanizing? These scenes may have been fun for Rich to write, and one or two may be necessary to give the reader a taste of the submariner's life: serious engineer by day, carefree young man traveling far from home, often for the first time, by night. But after mapping the elements on the target, it was evident that these scenes were creating an intermission from Rich's "one thing" that was overbearing.

Drawing the target helped illustrate how best to reduce unnecessary elements in future revisions and where the gaps were. Scenes from "the wild and crazy days" that were particularly fraught with ambiguity could stay. The characters who seemed to be internalizing the "1,000 Shades of Gray" the best, and acting out in distinct if inappropriate ways because of it, could stay. When something missed Rich's target, like an arrow lying on the ground, he was able to let it go. He didn't need it.

**Action Step #13: Draw the Target**

Draw a target and place your theme in the bull's-eye. Arrange each narrative element (scene, series, character, place) closer to or farther from the center based on its relevance to the theme.

## Find the Outliers

As we saw earlier, Rich had a well-honed theme, which allowed our class to place a number of elements closer to his bull's-eye rather than farther away. We observed that a number of his "good" scenes were clustered closer to the middle rather than being relegated to the periphery or—even worse—missing the target altogether. The challenge comes when you have to decide what is a worthy tangent and what is an *outlier*, which is the focus of our next action step.

Stefan was writing a great book on "the considered life," the benefits of making conscious choices in every conceivable area of life: work, food, art, our heroes, our lovers, and so on. One of his topics was religion. Stefan had strong ideas about religion. So strong that he put a forty-page play on the birth of our current Judeo-Christian way of thinking into the religion chapter. There was some good stuff in there, sure; but as his editor, I couldn't allow him to deform the overall unity of his book in this way.

This is where beta readers can come in so handy. If we decided that "Show, don't tell" is the most commonly heard expression in writing circles, then "Kill all your darlings" has to be in the top ten. The quote comes from William Faulkner: "In writing, you must kill all your darlings."* This phrase refers to the blind love you may feel for a particular part of your book—a love so strong that you may be blind to its obvious faults. If you receive a list of memorable scenes back from your beta readers, for example, and no one identified your favorite scene—it may be time to kill some darlings.

Stefan couldn't see his play lurking inside his work of philosophy. Rich couldn't see the 150 pages of ribald road stories lurking in his novel. Maybe they just weren't looking. When you train your eyes on your theme—when you accept that your book can only be about one thing—it is easier to see what material is tangential.

Now, not all tangential material is bad material. As Stefan would later say, "It has to be related, because it popped up. It is human to be spontaneous as opposed to preplanned. I don't want to be so didactic that I have to close every door."

Well said; let's see if we can find a compromise. Say Scene A connects to only one other scene, Scene B—but Scene B is well networked in the center of your target. Maybe Scene A can stay. Maybe Scene A is supporting material, a nice breather, comic relief, and illuminating in its own way. It is an objection that everyone will raise at some point in his or her work: "Why can't I keep this part even if it is not really related? What about the whimsical, the material that goes in, just because?"

---

* Faulkner got this from Sir Arthur Quiller-Couch: "Whenever you feel an impulse to perpetrate a piece of exceptionally fine writing, obey it—wholeheartedly—and delete it before sending your manuscript to press. Murder your darlings."

I'm not the most whimsical person on the planet, as you may have noticed. I'm more methodical (hence the Book Architecture *Method*), but I still faced this dilemma in writing this book. Some material that I really wanted to put in was related to only one other element on my target. It wasn't strictly necessary, but I liked it.*

You need to ask yourself, "Is this thought something that I want to keep, even if no one else presently appreciates its real value except me?" If so, you may have to stand up for its inclusion.

You may find that your question regarding tangential material runs more like this, however: "Is this grouping of scenes that didn't make the target actually more like a short story lurking inside a novel with a different theme?"

And then, of course, there is a third situation: material that is underutilized, that doesn't presently reflect the theme the way it could after a solid revision. You might give the tangential more attention, you might reduce its proportion, and you might eliminate it altogether. But first you have to find it.

### Action Step #14: Find the Outliers

Find the narrative elements that are the "outliers" on your target, either unrelated or only tangentially related to the others. If an element is tangential, you have some decisions to make about how important it could become. If an element is unrelated, you will need to either forge new connections or cut this material loose.

---

* I have often put this material into footnotes.

## Theme as an Essential Limiter

We have made a few allowances for keeping material that isn't 100 percent related to our theme. We are after structure here, not symmetry. That being said, I have to speak some words of praise for *limitation*.

People do not like to be limited. Limitation, however, is the key to revision—and nothing limits your action, your cast of characters, your proliferation of fabulous philosophic ideals, or your page count better than a good theme.

What can be limited? Pretty much anything you can think of:

- **Characters.** Both flat characters (those who do not evolve) and round characters (whose growth/deterioration we follow) can be limited. Every character needs to serve the theme, must represent an aspect of the theme. Nine and a half times out of ten, works in progress have too many characters for the reader to comfortably follow. Why not combine a bunch of people?*

- **Scenes.** This is an easy one. A little farther down the mountain, we will discuss how if you have three scenes doing the same thing, you can take the best parts of each and combine them into one uber-scene, which you

---

* If you are writing a memoir and are fearing the wrath of living people who are either in or out of your book (or not in it enough, or not in the right way), why not combine a bunch of people?

can then slot into the right place. We will also discuss when it is time to say good-bye once and for all to the "bad" or "forgotten" scenes.

- **Ideas.** Your book can only be about one thing. Right? It can be about the different ramifications of one thing . . . but that's it.

- **Series.** That's right—entire series can go. In Chapter Nine, we will confirm the intersection of your different series through the mechanism of the key scenes; if at that point, you still can't get a particular series to interact with the others, it may be time to cut it loose.

- **Twists and turns.** Some series arcs go up and down and up and down and up and down, until, yes, we're feeling a little sick. In fact, we don't know what to feel; we're bewildered. Why not streamline a series so we can have some idea of where we're going and that we've arrived?

- **Time-jumps.** In the next chapter, we discuss flashbacks and flash-forwards and how you can manipulate the timeline for psychological effect. While time-jumps can provide a pleasant mental challenge for the reader and help reveal your theme, just as often the book can be structured in a simpler way that is also more effective.

As Longinus said, "Genius needs the curb as often as the spur." I think he was talking about your genius!

In any event, remember: No matter how ideal your reader, he or she still has a finite attention span. In that case, what is your best chance of making an impact? Limitation.

Limitation is one aspect of revision. Some others we have explored in this chapter are realizing what you've actually written about, having the courage to continually improve what you are working on, and finding connections between tangential elements and the core of your work, your theme. It really is all about your theme. That is the solid ground from which you can continually view the road forward through your revision.

# Series,
# Part II

# Chapter Seven

# Beginnings, Middles, and Ends

At this point you have chosen a theme for your next revision. Your book can only be about one thing, and you know what you want it to be about. *How* to make a book about that is the focus of the next three chapters, which constitute "Series, Part II." We will continue scaling down the mountain by examining our individual series in greater detail and creating an overall scenic order in which every series interacts at the proper time. To do this we must learn a little more about working with series, and to do that we must first choose a *central series* to work with.

## Your Central Series

Which is your central series? The name *central series* may make you feel that the one you pick should be the most important one—but you may not know which one that is yet. Think of a series* that:

- **Orients your reader** to the general motion of your book. Up where? Down where? Ends about where? We have seen that there is not one narrative arc, but rather multiple narrative arcs that exist as individual series. The central series, however, usually best mirrors the overall sense of direction. (Look at the IDENTITY series on page 45 for an example.)

- **Lets the reader keep time.** By following this series, the reader knows which day it is (or year, if you are using flashbacks). In the next section, I will discuss some guidelines for returning your reader to the central series. For now, we'll just stress the importance of having one, what we might also call the *timekeeper series.*

- **Grounds the reader** in what is going on. What is at stake? What is the question? What are we talking about here, in its simplest terms? In "The Ugly Duckling," IDENTITY is the central series because it asks the big question: What is he? He doesn't come out of a turkey

---

*    The central series of this book is the journey up and down the mountain. It may have looked clumsy at first, like an oversimplification, but it serves its purpose to indicate direction and chart progress. Right?

egg . . . he's an unusually strong swimmer . . . You can ask yourself at certain times in the story, "Does he know yet?" Do *we* know yet?

Leyla's novel was about a band that traveled around and played different gigs in European cities. That wasn't her theme— she didn't know what her theme was at the time she took the class because she hadn't generated enough material yet. She did know her central series, however, and that actually helped her generate material, because she knew what was going to happen: A band travels around and plays gigs in different European cities. So now Scene A could happen in Stuttgart, Scene G could happen in Oslo, and so on.

The central series in Lori's novel was the quest to adopt a young Guatemalan girl, Anjel. You can imagine the iterations in this series: meeting Anjel, the head of Anjel's orphanage rising up in opposition to Lori's protagonist, trips to lawyers, getting visas and seals, paying money, paying more money . . . we can follow where we are in the novel because we know where Anjel is. Is she with her biological father? Is she getting on a plane to the United States with Lori, but only with a limited visa? That sort of thing.

Lori's central series was the adoption of Anjel, and knowing this allowed her to introduce effective twists and turns, including a surprise ending in which the adoption comes through at the same time that the new mom and daughter are separated, never to reunite. The emotional richness of this development is possible only because we know what is going on.

> **Action Step #15: Your Central Series**
>
> Choose a series that reflects the basic timeline of your work, one that your reader can identify and track. You will use this central series first in each of the next three steps to learn tools that you can then apply to all of your other series.

## Narrative Order vs. Chronological Order

Once you have selected your central series, the first decision you will have to make is whether you want to put it in *narrative order* or in *chronological order*. Let's start with chronological order. In chronological order, events happen one after another in time: today, tomorrow, next year. "The Ugly Duckling" is reported in chronological order. There are no flashbacks, flash-forwards, or multiple timelines.

Narrative order means the events are not presented in the order in which they happened. There are good reasons to do this—and as we will see in the next section, there are not-so-good reasons to do this. To some degree, this is the natural way to tell a story: reorganizing what happened into a different order to make a particular impact.

Say you are out on a date. You just got out of a long-term relationship, and your new love interest asks you about it. The chronological order of events might have gone like this:

1. Meeting Unexpectedly
2. Falling in Love
3. Climax*
4. Falling Out of Love
5. The Breakup

You are probably going to tell the story of your last relationship using narrative order, because it has a psychological effect. You might start with (4) Falling Out of Love, and mention all the things you couldn't live with. You would probably go to (5) The Breakup, to assure your new friend that things are really over—although you might first go back to (2) Falling in Love, if you can find the clues of what was wrong with this previous person to bolster your argument, that foreshadowing of how the relationship was doomed.

So 4-2-5 . . . that's probably the story you are going to tell.†
That's the part that is of interest to your present audience. Each decision you make about order is related to what you want to communicate, and to whom.

If you use narrative order, you will likely avail yourself of the literary device known as the *flashback*. A flashback occurs when you leave the present timeline to recount something that happened previously, and then return to the same narrative timeline you were in before. Flashing back can help explain things—in fact, I think that's why we go to therapy! We're sitting there with a problem, and we think back; a previous scene provides our

---

\* In the Shakespearean sense—easy there.
† And a classic example of "withholding information"!

motivation and we feel better.* The past has provided us with some meaning. The temptation to flash back in your writing is strong; it is a kind of instant gratification that may or may not be oversimplifying things.

If you are going to arrange your central series in narrative order, let me offer the following general guidelines to keep your reader with you while you do:

1. When we flash back, we do so for a reason, which is revealed to the reader eventually. This "reveal" can be subtle, but since every narrative element must belong to the theme, readers need to be able to make some kind of connection.

2. We don't leave the present time period for so long that the reader loses his or her bearings upon our return. In other words, we don't fall in love with another time period and dally there, favoring it over the present.

3. We don't flash back for too short a time, such as a few lines or a paragraph, which is really more like recovering a memory. Better to stay in the present in that case and recount the past events through a character's thoughts. When we do flash back, it should be for an entire scene.

---

* Just as flashbacks work because they correspond with our psychology, flash-forwards—jumping forward in narrative order—usually don't work because the human psyche is not constructed that way. If someone asks about your past, you can discourse on it rather freely even though you might end up changing the subject. If someone asks about the future, though, all but the most reckless souls will admit they don't know yet.

4. Information in the "past" (relative to the present time period) is contained in scene, with all of the benefits a scene creates: immediacy, reality, and suspense. This doesn't mean a flashback can be only one scene long; it can be longer provided readers aren't lost upon their return (see guideline 2).

Earlier, we were speaking about how complexity comes from the intersection and interaction of various series, not from individually complex series. When individual series are too complex, the overall design is unlikely to escape confusion. By this logic, if your book is using multiple timelines, you may have good reason to keep each of them individually in chronological order.

> **Action Step #16: Chronological Order vs. Narrative Order**
>
> Establish whether your central series will be presented in chronological order or narrative order. Make this decision for each of your major series. Remember: If your central series will be in narrative order, it may aid the reader to present many of your other series in chronological order.

## Begin at the Beginning

By deciding whether our series will be in chronological or narrative order, we come down the mountain by a different path than the one we used to ascend. In the next action step we will continue further down until we rescue all of those cut-up scenes from Action Step #5. We are going to put everything together again, thoughtfully. Ninety-nine good scenes in the right order, remember?

Let me first clear something up. Writers are often taught to begin *in medias res*, a Latin term that is often mistranslated as "in the middle." (It actually means "into the middle of things," as we will discuss shortly.) Unfortunately, this misconception has led to so many books nowadays actually beginning in the middle, with a lone, out-of-sequence scene that is supposed to provide the bulk of the foreshadowing. Then we go back in the narrative timeline, and every other event is presented chronologically.

I'm not saying this can't work; I'm just saying that it's not the only way to start a story. Imagine if "The Ugly Duckling" had been written in today's style. We would get him dreaming in the marsh, lying among the rushes when he sees three royal birds (swans) and rushes at them to end his own life. "But why?" the reader would ask. "Why would he want to do such a thing?" We would have this hanging over our heads throughout the rest of story, which might create some interest, but I feel it would also overdirect our expectations, and the process of improvement or deterioration that might naturally unfold regarding the little duckling's fate would constantly be skipping forward to this moment.

I understand why writers want to do this. The pressures of the marketplace being what they are, you need to grab the reader in *x* number of pages. But the reading experience usually does not benefit from just a little bit of narrative order. There are other ways to establish tension and interest. As I mentioned, *in medias res* does not mean "in the middle"—it means "into the middle of things." It means begin with a scene where there is something happening, and because of that something changes. This is sometimes called an *inciting incident* or *the springs of an action*.

Why not begin at the beginning? Why not begin with a mystery egg somehow ending up in a duck's nest? I think that generates enough interest, as it is poked and prodded. There's a question; something is unfinished.

You never get a second chance to make a first impression. When deciding which iteration to put first in your central series, pick one where you can move quickly into the action of a scene, where a relationship is already established, something that will set the tone. Bear in mind, you may not have written it yet. That's the nature of a draft: We write our way in, turning up interesting material as we go—then we go back through our series to fill in the missing iterations, whether they are in the beginning, the middle, or the end.

## The Missing Middle

Chances are, the middle is where you are missing the most iterations. This could be because you haven't figured out how your individual series will intersect and interact (which I will discuss in the next chapter). Or it could be because you haven't effectively charted new variations to the repetitions within a given series, such as additional complications for characters, red herrings that will throw off the investigation, and so on.

Let's examine the latter of these. In the central series of "The Ugly Duckling," we get an egg whose IDENTITY is a mystery. It's not a turkey's egg. The ugly duckling is a beautiful swimmer. Some wild ducks come right out and ask him, "What kind of a creature are you?" Each iteration builds on the one before it, and this is how you get through the missing middle, or the "murky middle," as it is sometimes called. By keeping the questions clear, we can keep some answered while some remain unanswered. The questions progress and some expectations are satisfied while new ones arise. As Louis Catron said, "When the questions are answered, the play is over."

An end to our questions is an end to your narrative, which readers will need at some point. At the same time, readers want the questions to unfold slowly; they want things to play themselves out. I have seen writers with a missing middle simply take the end and attach it to the beginning. (What middle?) Maybe this is related to our current attention span; we want things quicker, especially our middles. But there is a difference between speeding up the pace of reading (Chapters Eight and Nine in this book, for example, are the shortest of the main chapters, creating acceleration) and skipping the climax or its immediate effects.

Besides, if your series have been charted effectively, the middle can't be wrapped up that quickly; we'll return to this in the next chapter. Most readers will give you the first sixty pages, or even a hundred—especially if they paid for your book. They will give you the last sixty pages, because, hey, they got this far. But for them to navigate the middle, you have to create a clear pathway through the limitation of extraneous elements. At the same time, however, complications must arise—the introduction of new information that readers are only beginning to understand is what makes that pathway interesting. If this sounds difficult, it is at least the same difficulty that comes with personal maturation. The middle is where short stories grow up to be books. Many people think it is the beginning, or setup, that determines whether something is a short story or a novel; it isn't. It's how many series are involved and how well they come together.

## How Not to End Things

I can't tell you how to end your book—or your central series, which many times are one and the same. I can categorize types of endings for our review. I can admit a certain fondness for the *open-ended ending*: an ending where gestures are symbolic enough, where the words spoken are applicable enough that they mean something to us—even if we don't necessarily seek to impose that meaning on other people. As Chloe said, "I still have not recovered from reading the ending of *Gone with the Wind* when I was thirteen. I think encountering an open-ended ending represents the first steps toward adulthood from childhood. You mean, things in life don't always work out?"

Unfortunately, it is easier to talk about how not to end things, at least at first. We have all struggled with how to end things, whether it be a particular series or an entire work. There are so many pitfalls! Having made all of these mistakes myself, I offer the following categorization of how not to end things—with the caveat that if you can think of a convincing reason to ignore me in the case of your particular book, you should go ahead:

• **The speech-that-reveals-all ending.** This is what my students had a problem with in "The Ugly Duckling." At the very end everything is laid out for us: "He was very happy, but not all proud, for a good heart never becomes proud." Where is the ambiguity? Where can readers respond with what they are feeling or how they interpret the events?

• **The overly obscure ending.** This is the opposite of the speech-that-reveals-all ending. An author may not want to deliver explicit judgment on who was right or wrong, but readers still need to be able to get a clear fix on the events themselves, the scenes in which the end happens.*

• **The horrifying-end-that-awaits-us-all ending.** The novelist John Irving loves to do this. Take every series of events and just head it down the toilet. Sometimes we can fall into the trap that utter darkness is how we should end our tale. I'm not suggesting that your ending

---

* A poet once ended a novel with a word that no one knew. By forcing people to go to a dictionary, he thought it would be cool to have readers closing one book and opening another. Um, no.

should be overly light. I think as readers we're just asking for an ending that befits the rest (see the *spirit-of-fair-play ending* following this list).

- **The abrupt, that's-what-it-is ending.** This is what I was referring to in the "missing middle" section earlier. The very, very end stuck onto the middle of the middle. We think we're appealing to people's shrinking attention spans, but our readers get a feeling that they have finished the race ahead of us . . . and maybe they cheated?

- **The irresponsible ending.** This is a variation of Picasso's mug:* "My characters are stronger than me," writers say. "I can't say why it happened, it just did." The problem with this kind of ending is that everything we create, especially the ending, is an act of projection that clearly identifies our values for all to see.

Now that we have looked at what not to do, how can we feel our way into what we want to do? I mentioned the open-ended ending, and that is what I have tried to do with this book in the conclusion. We might also consider something known as the *spirit-of-fair-play ending.* In this type of ending, series that we have come to understand unfold into a just finale. Series meet other series and predictable things happen, or unpredictable but

---

* "Painting is stronger than I am. It makes me do what it wishes."—from Chapter Five.

J.D.'s scenes on different-colored Post-it notes that
represent her series. What's with that space at the end?

logical things happen, and those intersections occur more quickly
toward the end—and sometimes all at once. In the spirit-of-fair-
play ending, readers get the feeling that what happens is what is
supposed to happen, because, bear in mind, the way you end
your central series, and by extension all of your series, will communicate your value system. If someone dies in a car accident,
you are implying either that they deserved it or that the world is
a brutal and unpredictable place. If a couple falls in love, you are
implying that love is possible. When an end is proving particularly difficult, it may be that we do not want to own up to our
own position on the matter.

Of course, you may not have written the end yet. Missing
scenes can come from anywhere: the beginning, the middle, or
the end. Or you may really be done. One of the most magical
moments ever in class was when J.D. arranged each of her series
on different-colored Post-it notes that all flowed over a giant
piece of poster board like a lazy river. Up and down, a few eddies
for interest, but basically the overall flow was smooth. Then J.D.

pointed to the part of the poster board that she thought held the end she still wanted to write. She had left it blank, thinking she had to write "the end." But when she started talking about what the next iterations in each of her series were going to be . . . there really weren't any. That was how it felt to have charted out every useful iteration of each series. She was done.

> **Action Step #17: Beginnings, Middles, and Ends**
>
> Examine the beginning, middle, and end of your central series to determine where you may be missing an iteration, or where you have iterations without effect. Then examine each of your major series in the same way, looking at the segments of their individual arcs.

# Chapter Eight

# How Many Iterations Should I Have?

The title of this chapter is a variation of questions we have asked before: "How many scenes should I have?" Or, "How many series should I have?" I can't answer your question, "How many iterations of a given series should I have?" because (a) this is a method, not a formula, and (b) I haven't read your book.* I do think, however, that we can make some general observations about the number of iterations you will choose, because every decision has consequences and its own kind of rationale. By the end of this chapter you will have gone through each of your major series and determined how many iterations each of them should have—this is the work that prepares us for the final effort of knotting series together in Chapter Nine.

---

* Although if you've gotten this far in the method, I'll bet it's going to be good.

## One Iteration: "The Cameo"

There really is no such thing as one iteration of a series. This almost goes without saying; a series by definition has to have something repeat and vary. If it occurs only once, we won't have a sense of its direction—and the direction of a series is what gives it its meaning. Yet when we go through our work we find (much to our dismay) several one-iteration series: series that never went anywhere, that we lost interest in or simply forgot about. The question we need to ask ourselves then is, *"Expandable* or *expendable?"* Do we want to make more out of this series, or are we content to have it disappear—because that is the fate of all one-iteration series?

Let me try to prove it to you. In class, when we brainstorm one-iteration series, we come up with terms like *cameo* or *red herring*. A cameo occurs when we recognize a famous actor who appears only once in the film we are watching. But the fact that we recognize him or her at all indicates that there is a preceding iteration, just not in this picture. A red herring is a clue designed to throw us off the track when we are reading a detective novel. It disappears in a matter of pages, but we still need two iterations: the one where we think we've got something, and the one where that belief is discredited.

A one-iteration series doesn't exist. When something occurs for the first time, it establishes the context. The first time we encounter something, it goes straight into our subconscious. Only subsequent iterations bring out the meaning of this foreshadowing. Without a second iteration, something may happen, but nothing can really change—and thus in the end, we will fail to notice it.

Let's refresh the first three definitions of scene:

**A scene is where something happens.**

**A scene is where something changes.**

**A scene is related to the theme.**

I told you there were five definitions of scene total, and I think this is a good place to introduce number four:

**A scene is capable of series.**

Because readers have a limited ability to track information, writers need to apply that same concept of limitation to their own work. But you would be surprised by the number of elements that are written in a scene that are never repeated: characters, places, hot topics of discussion—these one-iteration series hanging out there. The vibrant café owner with caustic wit but a heart of gold: Where did he go? Or that cabin that seemed so mysterious: How come we never went back there? What was that about? Looking at your target, these one-iteration series are likely either arrows that missed the mark entirely or those "just-because" elements we encountered in Chapter Six. *Expandable* or *expendable*? One-iteration series are usually the latter.

## Two Iterations: "Identity and Change"

Back in our early work on series, we heard about Chekhov's gun—hanging on the wall in the first act, it goes off in the third act. The identity of the gun has been established, and now there is a change in its state. I like thinking about this prop because as anyone who has worked in theater can attest, budgets are limited. We don't have a thousand guns lying around backstage. If you want someone to be shot, you better use this gun, here. In writing your book, you might want to put yourself on a budget, for unity's sake. Just as in drama, you can have settings, costumes, characters, actions—just not an endless supply of them.

Two iterations is the most basic form of a series: something from the first iteration repeats in the second iteration, while at the same time it varies. But this doesn't mean that having only two iterations is bad or an undeveloped choice.

Consider the appearance of the swans in "The Ugly Duckling." There are only two iterations of the swan series: in scene five they appear remote and incomprehensible; in scene six the protagonist rushes at them trying to achieve obliteration but ends up in acceptance.

Changing the identity of something only once can still have vast implications for the meaning of your story. Or it could be that what you change is something small yet still satisfying to us as readers—we were able to identify what something was and how it changed, and that change propelled the narrative forward and increased our interest in what was happening.

On the other hand, if you have only two iterations of a series, you may find that you are missing the beginning, the middle, or the end. You may have the beginning and middle together, with the end separate, or you may have the middle and end clumped together, with the beginning separate. This is a case where you have iterations that are expandable as opposed to expendable. Can you profitably divide a series to allow for more development? This is sometimes known as *unpacking the meaning*, and it is what your readers are doing all the time, with or without your help. So let's help them—and in turn we will be helping ourselves, by giving ourselves more relevant material that can interact as the work takes on a richer complexity.

## Three Iterations: "Conflict, Crisis, and Resolution"

The number three has a magical kind of appeal. It is tempting to make every series have three iterations: the setup, the event, and the new situation. This three-iteration structure is so basic to our understanding of structure that we have pretty much accepted a plot as conflict, crisis, and resolution.

In many ways conflict, crisis, and resolution looks similar to the structure of this book. You go up the mountain, you reach the top, you go down the mountain. When you have three iterations you can actually change course, as opposed to simply showing a starting and ending point. This, incidentally, is where the term *narrative arc* really comes from. If you have two points, you

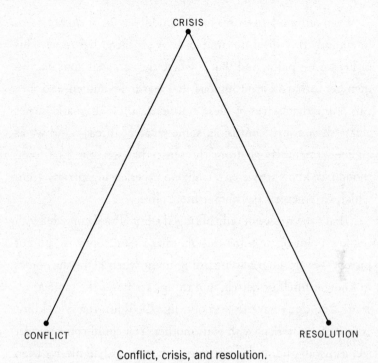

Conflict, crisis, and resolution.

can only make a line. You can bend that line, however, into an arc with this third, middle point.

Now it is tempting to make everything happen at that exact middle, and this is certainly the lore that has been passed down. The Greeks called the middle the *peripeteia*, or reversal. Aristotle defined this seminal iteration as "a change by which the action veers round to its opposite, subject always to our rule of probability or necessity."* As it turns out, its importance cannot be overstated.

---

* Probability or necessity, love it.

Even our modern words for the middle, *crisis* or *climax*, seem to embody this all-or-nothing ideal. A character has to have his or her lowest point, and that is where the catharsis appears. Remember catharsis: arousing pity and fear in an audience so they can purge themselves of these emotions. These dramatic scenes create discomfort, confusion, some sense of threat—and we as audience members go from the sense that we were fine (even though we know we weren't, really) to experiencing anxiety, from which we emerge a percentage more alive.

That's the work not only of tragedy, but also of comedy (with the low point being some mistake that isn't recognized) and of history—every hero has a turning point when he or she comes to know himself or herself, and things are never the same afterward. You don't have to find out, like Oedipus, that you killed your father and slept with your mother. You could come to realize, as Molly did at age six, that your parents had always been pot dealers, that in fact you lived on a pot farm.

Of course there can be multiple ups and downs, as we will see further on in this chapter. You can go up and further up. You can go down at the last moment and not return. My only point here is that without a third iteration of an individual series, you cannot have up-and-down at all. Earlier we examined the principle of *Use it, don't include it* (and its corollary, *If you're going to include, use it*). In the context of a three-iteration series, we can develop this further:

If you got it once, use it twice—three times is a charm.

## Four Iterations: "One, Two, Three, Many"

In his exploration of mathematical and scientific concepts, George Gamow reported that the "Hottentots" (Khoikhoi) only had words for "one," "two," "three," and "many." Dramatically speaking, we're still there. What is the difference between four iterations in a series and eleven iterations? Not very much. Yes, we can only enjoy the effects of suspense and surprise (as outlined in Chapter Four) when several iterations are present; yes, for variation to occur we usually must have multiple instances of repetition. My only point here is that from a macro perspective, our mind carries the magic of three and lays it onto whatever is unfolding.

The UGLINESS series, for example, has twelve iterations of ugly (ugly, monstrous, ugly, ugly, ugliness . . . ) before we get to the middle. The middle is only one iteration, the turning point (UGLINESS[13]: "I will fly to them, the royal birds, and they will hack me to pieces because I, who am so ugly, venture to approach them"). The end is composed of two iterations that make up resolution (the duckling is no longer ugly and ungainly; in fact, he is young and handsome!).

The point is that after three iterations, readers are set up for any number of iterations in a series, be it four, seven, or seventeen iterations. Because readers want to remember the beginning at the end (and ideally have the beginning reflected in the end), they hold both the beginning and the end in one hand, as it were, and stretch out the additional iterations like a longer and longer rope in the other hand. That's what we can handle.

## Five Iterations: The Shakespearean Stamp of Approval

In an analysis of Shakespeare's plays, Gustav Freytag expanded the three-part structure we have been studying, *conflict-crisis-resolution*, into a five-part structure:

- exposition

- rising action

- climax (or turning point)

- falling action

- denouement

While it seems like new stages have been added, Freytag's pyramid is really just further evidence of how we stretch the middle to include more and more iterations. Instead of beginning (exposition), middle (climax), and end (denouement), we have now added a beginning/middle (rising action) and a middle/end (falling action). It remains as true for Shakespeare as it does for us—because the middle is the furthest point that the audience has to travel, it is the most difficult and potentially rewarding of all of the sections of a narrative.

Earlier I said that a complex book does not come from complex series that are difficult to navigate. Complexity comes from

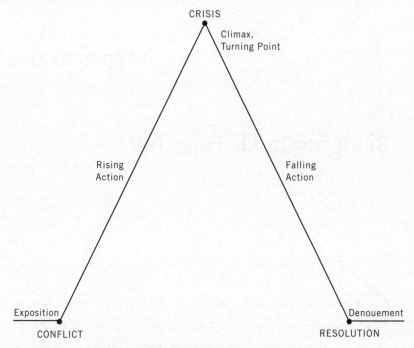

Conflict, crisis, and resolution . . . and a bunch
of other stuff.

clear, meaningful series that intersect and interact in meaningful ways (which is the focus of the next chapter). You can have as
many iterations in a given series as you want. I'm just recom-
mending again the power of keeping it simple.

### Action Step #18: Numbers of Iterations

Establish how many iterations will make up your central series and where the turning point(s) lie. Make this
decision for each of your major series, assessing whether
you need to have multiple ups and downs.

## Chapter Nine

# Bringing It All Together

Optimistic title, huh? Wait, there's more optimism. We have now arrived at the place where we will put all of our scenes in order. How do we do this? On the way up, we made the initial transition from scene to series via our key scenes, and we will use key scenes again to make our transition on the way down.

Let us cast a glance one more time at the key scene in "The Ugly Duckling." "I will fly to them, the royal birds, and they will hack me to pieces because I, who am so ugly, venture to approach them." I'll bet you almost have it memorized by now. The UGLINESS series ("I am so ugly") adjoins and fuels the PAIN/AGGRESSION series ("they will hack me to pieces") because of a mistaken IDENTITY (they are "royal birds," and I am not)—but at least we won't have the WEATHER series to contend with ("suffer so much misery in the winter").

A key scene brings two or more major series together. Series

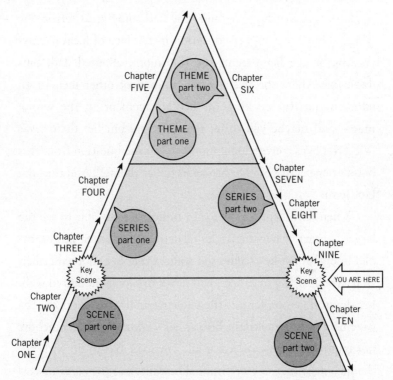

Transitioning from series to scene, through the key scene.

are never the same after they interact; to bring two series (or more) together is to have them inform each other by their very proximity. It is where, as they say, that the plot thickens. The key scene in "The Ugly Duckling" brings all of the major series together. "Easy for him," you might say. "His story has only one key scene, and my book has a dozen or more." One key scene at a time, my friend. When in doubt, narrow your focus. Spend some time thinking about one key scene at a time, and the rest will fall into place.

Jenn was writing a memoir. She had some great series: one where she pursues higher education in the face of local naysayers; one where her parents die (bio-mom, adopted dad, bio-dad); one where she sleeps with a bunch of other men in an effort to justify breaking off her engagement to the wrong man—and maybe you think that's wrong, but her theme was "victories over conventional morality," so the question from this book's perspective is, "Do her series fit her theme?" And they do. Go, Jenn.

When Jenn kept her theme in mind, she was able to see the larger context of how her series related to each other. For example, in one of her key scenes she realizes that her adopted father, Bob, who is dying of cancer, will never live long enough to walk her down the aisle. Jenn is then able to finally break off her engagement because without Bob at her wedding, she is somehow not required to get married at all. The logic has to do with her theme (victories over conventional morality); as the narrator says about the timing of Bob's heartbreaking demise, "My misfortune was a blessing that I couldn't share."

Picture your series as individual ropes and yourself as binding two (or more) ropes into a knot at each key scene. How much of each rope do you need before the knot? Let's take the key scene where Jenn breaks off her engagement. What needs to happen in each series leading up to this scene? The BUNCH OF OTHER MEN series needs some "events" that have her unfortunate fiancé Ali waiting up later and later for a woman who isn't coming home; Jenn now knew to place each of those scenes before the key scene in question. In the ALL MY PARENTS ARE DYING series, the rope that stretches out behind the key scene features Bob, unfortunately, getting cancer. And scenes in which his cancer gets worse.

If your book is about one thing, your series will encounter each other naturally. By observing where your series interact, you can put your key scenes in order first, then follow that up with a complete list of all of your scenes. The optimism returns.

There are some practical considerations for ordering key scenes in a way that will allow your series to inform each other at the right time, but if you ever get stuck, just examine what you've already done. If the question is, "How do I make this happen?" the answer might be found in, "How did I put this together?" It is okay to answer your own question with a question. Your previous draft may turn out to be your own best teacher.

The three practical considerations for ordering your key scenes are as follows:

1. What needs to happen, and by when?
2. What needs to have not happened yet?
3. Things need to continue to happen.*

Using these considerations, you are now ready to conquer the next action step, which is really a monumental step, and I recommend feeling a great deal of satisfaction as you complete it.

---

* As in, every scene has to have something happen, every scene has to have something change, and so on.

**Action Step #19: Order Your Key Scenes**

Put your key scenes in the order in which you want to present your material. By now you have all of the necessary information to make this decision.

## A Period of Absence

The first thing you will notice as you begin ordering your key scenes is that just as a lot of things are happening, a lot of things are not happening. They have been temporarily removed from the reader's perspective.

We are always holding back on several series at any given point in time. If everything happened at once, it would explode the space-time continuum of your book. Books don't work like that, for the same reason that time doesn't work like that—both books and time have to be linear for our minds to comprehend them.

While you're holding back on a particular series, why not have a reason at the same time? Take advantage of the period of absence, in other words, to withhold information along the lines of the following (by way of recap):

- **Suspense:** A series recurs regularly enough that we know we don't know something; readers are aware that they are missing some piece of critical information (e.g., *What kind of a creature is the ugly duckling?*).

- **Surprise:** A series occurs irregularly, so that we both remember the question and get the answer in the same moment (e.g., *Swans? Who said anything about swans?*).

- **Shock:** All but one iteration of a series are at least partially buried yet still clearly related to the narrative (e.g., *I guess it would make sense that ducks could get shot in this story*).

- **Foreshadowing:** A series is presented earlier in the narrative so that it is planted in the reader's subconscious mind but can easily be swept from the reader's conscious mind (e.g., *From the title on, the main character's ugliness is presumed*).

These techniques can be used to create a period of absence within a particular series. It is one of those mysteries that by not revealing something, you actually speed up the reader's pace. Withholding information—as a general category that includes these four techniques—increases the dramatic tension and helps get those pages turned.

## Order All of Your Scenes

In the next action step, you will order all of your scenes. Ninety-nine scenes in order, from one to ninety-nine.* I find two things

---

\* Not ninety-nine, really; you know the drill by now.

helpful to do at this point, and the first is for you to read the next chapter on links and segmentation. Familiarizing yourself with that information makes this step a little more intuitive. (I know, the fact that I can't give you all of the information at once is annoying to me too.)

The next thing I find helpful is to create order in smaller batches. These slightly messy groups look like a vast improvement over every scene being alone. "Does this scene belong to this group or that group?" is probably a question you can answer now. Once you have divided your scenes into groups, you can sort through each group, moving them around until they click. Remember to include your ideas for missing scenes. (We'll address bad and forgotten scenes in the next step.)

In this step your job is to put every scene you want to keep into a provisional order. It's better than your best guess—it's your informed opinion. Will you get your entire order right? While I would love to promise you that, I think the truth is more comforting—during your next draft, if a scene is out of place, it will be vastly more obvious than it was in your previous draft. It will practically walk up to you and, while not being able to speak, will gesture somewhat impatiently as to where it should go. Trust me.

### Action Step #20: Order All of Your Scenes

Assign all of your scences a number in the new order you will use going forward in your next draft. This is a big step, which paradoxically is best done quickly.

## Fate of the Bad and Forgotten Scenes

I think the most important skill a writer has to have is the ability to make decisions, and to be able to live with those decisions. I'm not sure if that's two skills or one. Let's go with one.

We have been waiting on the fifth and last definition of scene:

**A scene is where something happens.**

**A scene is where something changes.**

**A scene is related to the theme.**

**A scene is capable of series.**

Well, here it is:

**A scene has "it."**

Now you may think I'm kidding. I'm serious. A bad or forgotten scene that you keep while putting together your provisional scenic order has to really have a good shot at making it into your final draft. How do you know?

Because it has "it."

You may not know what "it" is, but you can still detect it; it resonates. Certain situations remind you of a given scene; you can't quite shake it. The scene has "it"—not that it's perfect. I don't think we should be above talking in ways like this, by the way; sometimes I think the situation demands it.

> **Action Step #21: Fate of the Bad and Forgotten Scenes**
>
> Examine each bad and forgotten scene and decide whether it is worthy of your next draft. You may decide that you just cannot drag those scenes any further. Revision is a process by which things get combined, shortened, or expanded. It is also a process by which certain things get left out.

# Scene,
# Part II

# Chapter Ten

# Links and Segmentation

We have now arrived at the bottom of the mountain, on the other side. From here you will prepare for further adventure—the writing of your next draft! We have one last thing to sort out, however, and that is how your work will be organized, not only in an overall sense, but within and among chapters. The two chief tools we will use to complete the task of organization are *links* and *segmentation*.

A *link* is a transitional passage that fuses one scene to another. *Segmentation* refers to the parts into which a narrative is divided: book chapters, theatrical acts, mini-series episodes, and so on. Within any given part, certain scenes are *linked* together, and that group of scenes is then *segmented* from all other groups of scenes. Thus, a group of scenes (what we call a chapter) can also be looked at as a *scenic run*.

The urge to put certain scenes together has existed all along. Back in Chapter Two, when we cut up all of your scenes, we lost all of your previous organization: We exploded your chapters and lost their numbers and funny/fancy titles (if they had them). We were left with only scenes. You might have thought that was a bummer then, but when you pushed your scenes into groups in Action Step #20, you may have had some revenge. Some of your scenes that adjoined each other in the original order have come back together again. As I mentioned, you may want to work back and forth between the material presented here and the last chapter to attain your final scenic order.

## Segmentation

Let's begin with segmentation, because it is a little more straightforward. When you pull all the way back and look at it, every narrative has a hierarchy of organization. You could start from something as small as a word. Words make a sentence, sentences make a paragraph, paragraphs make a page *and* a scene, and so on.

If you look at the following chart, you will see that we have put chapter after scene. A scene may be its own chapter, but more likely a chapter consists of a run of three to seven scenes. Not every scene can be its own chapter or we lose a sense of the rhythm of the book—it's just one thing after another; the pacing is flat. I don't want to be programmatic on the other hand and

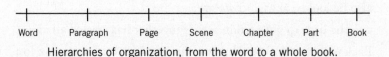

Hierarchies of organization, from the word to a whole book.

tell you how many scenes should be in a chapter or how many chapters you should have,* but I do think we should spend some time discussing the way the attention span works.

We've all flipped to the end of a chapter to see how many pages we have left. Maybe we have to get off an airplane, or we want to go to sleep. What we are looking for is that break when we can take a really deep breath—or, if we are really gripped by the narrative, when we can begin a new chapter, feeling enough momentum to carry us forward.

The breath, or break, that segmentation provides does three things:

- It allows what just happened to sink in; we grasp details better when given time to process them.

- It reconnects us to our present surroundings—which is paradoxically of benefit, allowing us to continue our reading rejuvenated.

- It gives us a taste of unity; each chapter has its own beginning, middle, and end, prefiguring the satisfaction we will have at the end of the book.

I hope I have convinced you of the value of segmentation. If you are a writer practicing contemporaneously with the publication of this book, you are probably used to the idea of

* Industry wisdom today states that you should have ten twenty-page chapters. How could they know that?

segmentation; as I note in the section on *white space* that follows, we seem to get a lot of it these days. What we seem to have lost focus on is the value of links.

## Links

One of the most commonly heard expressions in writing circles is "the willing suspension of disbelief." Coined by S. T. Coleridge, it has become a kind of gold standard by which we measure literary works. Coleridge asked in essence, does the reader suspend judgment concerning the plausibility of a narrative?

They want to, or they wouldn't be reading. The reader agrees to refrain from asking certain kinds of questions (e.g., "Did this really happen?") provided certain other kinds of questions don't come up (e.g., "That couldn't really happen, could it?")

Readers have agreed to play by the rules of your game. They will follow along with you . . . until you get them lost. When they start looking around for someone who knows where they are going, then you have a problem.

The way to solve this problem is through links, because links establish logic. Maybe there is a temporal succession between scenes, or a causal connection, or you have provided some other reasoning why something should come next and something should come after that.

I choose the word *link* because of the image of the chain, and the old saying that "the strength of the chain is no greater than that of the weakest link." A weak link will cause your reader's attention to wander at best, and snap at worst. A strong link will establish your skill beyond a reasonable doubt and preserve the willing suspension of disbelief.

## The "Natural Cycle" Link

We will explore several different kinds of links in this chapter. These narrative passages can range from a phrase to several pages in length; they can be introverted or extroverted, in terms of how much attention they bring to themselves. On the introverted end of the spectrum, the least daring links are the ones in which the least amount changes. Remember Aristotle's three unities: unity of place, unity of time, unity of action (theme)? What if you changed only one of them between scenes?

An example of this would be the *"natural cycle" link*. Andersen uses it between scene one and scene two of "The Ugly Duckling":

Next day was gloriously fine, and the sun shone on all the green dock leaves . . .

That's it; nothing elaborate. The place didn't change, the idea hasn't developed substantively, it's just one day later. Andersen does it again between scene two and scene three:

So the first day passed, and afterwards matters grew worse and worse . . .

In nonfiction the equivalent is simply saying, "When we turn to the next chapter, we will discuss A, B, and C." Later we'll discuss objections as to whether such a thing is necessary. For now, let's just observe this simplest form of a link: changing only the time. In the natural cycle link things grow or wither, the season changes, the sun rises. There's nothing wrong with that. It happens every day.

## The "Transportation" Link

Andersen uses a variety of natural cycle links, and we find another one between scene three and scene four, except this time we also encounter a change of place:

> Towards night he reached a poor little cottage.

You might say that this link actually begins a few sentences earlier, when the change of place is put most heavily into motion; unlike simply changing the time, a change of place usually requires some words to get us from here to there. I call this kind of link the *transportation link*. The full text of the link between scene three and scene four in "The Ugly Duckling" reads:

> . . . and then he hurried away from the marsh as fast as he could. He ran across fields and meadows, and there was such a wind that he had hard work to make his way.
> Towards night he reached a poor little cottage.

In the case of this book, we have marked our transitions through the narrative by the visual metaphor of traveling up and down a mountain. One of the advantages of the mountain as a central series is that it lends itself very well to transportation links: "By deciding whether our series will be in chronological or narrative order, we come down the mountain by a different path than the one we used to ascend. In the next action step we will continue further down until we rescue all of those cut-up scenes. . . ." There you go; section on chronological order, meet section on beginnings.

We've all seen examples of the transportation link in workshops. The character gets on the bus. While traveling through his city, he observes both the people on the bus and the passing surroundings. He gets off at his job. Whether we are traveling from scene to scene by camel or rocket blast, we can make use of some physical conveyance to get us there. The problem comes when we dally in the link itself—when we take the opportunity of being on the bus to have something the character sees trigger a series of thoughts that stretch further and further away from the scene. Remember one of our most basic injunctions: Everything has to happen in scene. Show, don't tell. There are times to tell, as we will see shortly. For now, let's agree that usually nothing that important happens on the bus. Use the transportation link to get from Scene A to Scene B, but use it wisely.

## The "Voice-Over" Link

So far we have seen links that change time and/or place. There are variations on this, such as in a novel where there is more than one point of view. Then you might go back in time and to another place to relate what a different character was experiencing, then come forward again with the new character in time. These are all still "introverted" links in terms of how much a link changes between two scenes. We get the more "extroverted" links when we start using our voice.

There comes a time when you just have to change the subject. I am doing that right now. We can call this the *voice-over link*. I am counting on our relationship, the one we have developed, to allow us to transition from that to this, what we're talking about now. Such communication appears to "break the fourth wall"—a theater reference for speaking across the stage directly to the audience. Yet just as in theater, enjoyment and engagement can occur in that way too.

All narratives start with some form of "Let me tell you a story." Now you're just saying, "Let me tell you the next part . . ." It doesn't have to rupture the willing suspension of disbelief if you are matter-of-fact about it. People don't obsess in conversation, they just skip along from scene to scene with a variety of tics: "The reason I called you is . . ." "Did I ever tell you about the time when I . . ." "Like I said before . . ." and then they follow up with nothing like what they were talking about.

Andersen uses the voice-over link between scene five and scene six in "The Ugly Duckling":

> But it would be too sad to mention all the privation and misery he had to go through during the hard winter.

It is what it is. The voice-over link is almost ornamental, in the sense of the gargoyles and other decorative elements you see on churches. I have heard that when the builders of such edifices reached a seam in their materials and couldn't effectively connect the viewer's perspective, instead of trying to distract their attention from that point, they hung something there instead. I have no idea if this true. At this point, I don't even want to know. In the true spirit of the voice-over link, it doesn't even matter. As the name *voice-over* indicates, it is your voice that will help you pull off this kind of link, ushering readers into the next scene.

## The "Representative Actions" Link

One other link I want to draw your attention to is the *representative actions link*. In this type of link, a summary is presented by showing symbolic events repeated over a period of time. It could cover the time that an injury heals, or a marriage finally falls apart, or a period where not very much happens except that things just naturally progress.

Andersen uses the representative actions link between scene five and scene six:

> So away went the duckling. He floated on the water and ducked underneath it, but he was looked at askance and was slighted by every living creature for his ugliness. Now autumn came. The leaves in the woods turned yellow and brown. The wind took hold of them, and they danced about. The sky looked very cold and the clouds hung heavy with snow and hail. A raven stood on the fence and croaked

"Caw, caw!" from sheer cold. It made one shiver only to think of it. The poor duckling certainly was in a bad case!

In the nineteenth century, a representative actions link was called a summary. Books were frequently stitched together *scene–summary–scene–summary–etc.* To summarize is potentially dangerous, however, where scene is concerned. Remember, "Show, don't tell." How do we show events even as they speed up, with all of the color, action, and feeling they deserve? The representative actions link invites us to distinguish *scene–representative actions link–scene* as something different than *show–tell–show*.

I will break with tradition here and use an example from a book that we haven't read in common. It is from Hermann Hesse's novel *Siddhartha*. (If we're going to break with tradition, we might as well enjoy it, right?) This passage occurs after Siddhartha has returned to the old ferryman, Vasudeva, whose services Siddhartha had employed much earlier in the novel. Now Siddhartha wants to learn how to become a ferryman too. That's all you need to know.

From that scene to the next we have a representative actions link:

And from one occasion to the next, [Siddhartha's] smile came more and more to resemble the ferryman's. It became nearly as radiant, nearly as aglow with happiness, shone in the same way out of a thousand little wrinkles, was just as much like a child's and just as much like an old man's. Many travelers, seeing the two ferrymen, took them for brothers. Often the two sat in the evening on the tree trunk on the bank and listened in silence to the river, which for them was not a river but the voice of life, the voice of what is, eternal becoming. And occasionally it happened that while listening to the river both men would think of the same thing—a conversation from the day before yesterday, one of their passengers whose face and fortune had caught their interest, of death, of their childhood; and then at the same moment, when the river had said something good to them, they would look at each other, both thinking exactly the same thing, both gladdened by the same answer to the same question.

Certain words and phrases mark this passage as a representative actions link: "from one occasion to the next," "often," "occasionally it happened." But the reader doesn't get the sense that a period of time is being summarized out of scene—we can still see the faces of the men, we can still hear the river and maybe even occasional laughter. Rather than simply resorting to flat telling, a representative actions link can combine the best of changing time and place with an authoritative voice that comforts or cajoles the reader.

## White Space, Asterisks, and Other Pretend Links

Speaking of cajoling (voice-over link), I have tried to do little of it in this book. But I'm going to go out on a limb here and ask that whichever links you choose, please do me a favor and use a bunch of them!

A fashion in writing today is to skip links, and in their place to put a row of asterisks like this:

* * *

. . . and then we're into the next scene. Sometimes, a block of extra white space (also known as a *space break* or a *crot*) is used to accomplish the same thing, and takes up about as much room. To wit:

. . . and the next scene begins with a different character, in a different place, concerned with something completely separate. Is it because the writer couldn't find the link? Is it to represent the indeterminacy of today's culture? Do we even know we are doing it?

The thing is, either you put the link there or your readers will put it there for you. If you give them enough information that they can guess why your scenes are in this order, and everything works out—that's great. But a link between scenes is designed to create continuity and enhance intensity.

One day I was leading a class on links—you know, those textual passages that combine scenes in a narrative. Someone said they were like connective tissue. I said that they could be between just a few words in length and several pages. Innocent stuff. I said:

"Instead of simply putting up a typographical fence or some empty white space when your flow dries up, can you find a link instead?"

This started what I came to call "The White Space Furor." The group erupted with objections:

"Those examples from 'The Ugly Duckling' are corny!"

"You haven't read Don DeLillo's book *Falling Man*!"

"MFA programs demand white space!"

"What about all these white spaces in this Langston Hughes poem?"

It was the whole table against me . . . good times! (Space in poetry acts more like punctuation in prose, by the way.)

Here's my point: In narrative, you have to be able to connect scenes. When you're telling someone a story face-to-face, you can't pause for a few seconds to indicate that some major shift has taken place. Actors aren't quiet on stage for a while during a scene. Filmmakers have developed at least twenty techniques for creating transitions; they call it editing. When there's "dead air" on the radio, we switch it off.

All I said was, I don't want to see a lot of white space. I didn't call it laziness; somebody else did. I'm just trying to get inside your head so that the next time you don't know what comes next, you think about what comes next. As readers, we don't know what comes next, either. Could you guide us in a way that doesn't bring too much anxiety?

**Action Step #22: Restore Links and Segmentation**

Each scene needs to be either linked to or segmented from the scene before it. Experiment with different kinds of links to create "scenic runs," or chapters. Once your chapters are established, you might title and/or number them to enhance their segmentation and create a clear road map for the reader.

# Conclusion:
# A Word on Unity

Way back in "Scene, Part I," I said: You can never achieve unity—the goal of any piece of writing—by trying to be comprehensive. You will always be missing something. I'm sure I'm missing something here; this book is not comprehensive. If it feels like it is (one can only hope), it's because the elements are well enough related. You don't ask too many questions for which the answer isn't also right there.

If we can't attempt to be comprehensive, what can we be? We can be *consistent*, we can be *coherent*, we can establish *continuity*. Maybe we don't even pursue unity, but instead we pursue the unity of something. The unity of scene. The unity of series, and so on. That is what this coda is about.

## Unity of Scene

Ninety-nine scenes in the right order, remember? Ninety-nine good scenes. Not one hundred—we're not reaching for that level of comprehensiveness. We just want to be consistent: all of the good, none of the bad. Something happens, and because something happens, something changes. In all of them. You will not be able to come up with everything that could possibly happen— you're going to have to take what comes to you and run with that.

## Unity of Series

Whatever the size of a particular arc, whether two iterations or seventeen iterations, the consistency-versus-comprehensive debate can be applied to series as well. Does a series have a beginning, middle, and an end? Is it the beginning, middle, and end of the same thing?

Do we really need to know about that, or can we live without it? And if we do need to know about it, do we need to know about it now? Withholding information, foreshadowing, suspense, surprise, shock—all our old friends—can help you craft individual series that balance expectation and satisfaction.

## Unity of Theme

This is an easy one; your book can only be about one thing. Since consistency doesn't apply when considering only one thing, we'll pull in our second description of unity: *coherence*. When something coheres, it means elements attach by a force like gravity to a center. Molecular structures cohere; so do planetary systems.

In our case, we have a target: concentric circles of the relevance of a piece of information, leading to a bull's-eye. Here is where we choose between keeping the tangential scene that we like and is loosely related, and letting go of the whimsical scene that doesn't really matter.

Your four-line thematic statement, your two-line version, and finally the one thing your book is about gives you that center. We're not talking about unity in the abstract; we're talking about the unity of something. We've cut down our lofty expectations and increased our chances of success in one fell swoop. Our scenes and our series are working together to one purpose.

## Unity of Links and Segmentation

We have seen that unity is consistency, and unity is coherence. Unity also establishes *continuity*, and that is the work of links and segmentation. Links are where we get the feeling not only that everything in your book belongs together (coheres), but that it belongs together in a certain order.

Your readers aren't looking only for holistic. They're also looking for linear. Your book is like one long formula, written beginning to end; we can only do the math one operation at a time. If you do manage to bring us full circle, back to the beginning, you may have achieved the ultimate expression of unity. But you're still going to have to do it one scene at a time, and that scene linked to the next scene. And so on . . .

## Indra's Net

There is a parable in Buddhism (via Hinduism) called "Indra's Net." Indra was originally a Vedic god who owned the most marvelous fishing net—in place of knots tying the individual pieces of rope together, there were jewels. Each jewel reflected every other jewel inside its twinkling eye—any change in one jewel was simultaneously reflected in all of the other jewels.

We've been tying some ropes in this book. Now we can consider each element of your book as a jewel: each internal thought, each location, each event. From a single line of dialogue to a complex series resulting in the evolution of a character, everything needs to relate to the whole and reflect it, or . . . your net is not godlike.

Which is okay! We do what we can do. To put forth a narrative that is satisfying and proportional, we start with the details. Mother Teresa said, "We cannot do great things. We can only do small things, with great love." But I first heard the idea from Stephen, my food and beverage manager when I was a waiter.

He said, "Here we take care of the little things. And we let the big things take care of themselves."

Once we are focused on the level of detail, and in a decision-making mode, then we remember the word that nobody likes: *limitation*. If I have convinced you that you cannot achieve comprehensiveness, which is accomplished by expansion, then what is the opposite of expansion? Limitation is the key to organization and revision.

I have more to say. I always will. But I don't want to contradict what I have put forth so far. Indra's net points us to one more kind of unity, the unity of unity, if you will. This means that your structure fits your theme—a family saga isn't short-story length, and a method for organizing and revising your material isn't a thousand pages long.

And besides, this book was about you, anyway. Here we are at the end for me, but it's just the beginning for you. You are now ready to go through your entire manuscript again and handle all of your material with confidence. That's not an action step; you've had enough of them. Knowing that your book can't be all things (to all people), you also have a much better idea of what you want it to be—what would be fun, what might mean something, what is interesting to you—and a pretty good idea of how you're going to go about pulling it off.

Let's get to it.

# Tools

# The Book Architecture Method: 22 Steps to Prepare Your Manuscript for Revision

## Action Step #1: Brainstorm Your Scenes

Make a list of every scene in your book without looking at your manuscript. Give each scene a name that will bring you quickly back to what happens there.

## Action Step #2: Your Good Scenes

Highlight the "good" scenes on your list in green, the ones that are done (for now). You are not looking for perfection, which is something different. These are the scenes that "work."

## Action Step #3: Your Bad Scenes

Highlight the "bad" scenes on your list in pink. Your bad scenes are the ones that cause you some anxiety, that nag at you—the ones that you did not nail.

## Action Step #4: Your Forgotten Scenes

Go back through your manuscript and identify your "forgotten" scenes. (After this step, your entire manuscript should be divided into scenes.) Give these scenes a name and highlight them in blue, but don't try to assess whether they are "good" or "bad." They are "forgotten."

## Action Step #5: Cut Up Your Scenes

Cut up all of your scenes, either by placing them into individual electronic files or by using scissors and a stapler. This is a radical act that will free your future revision from being a mere derivation of your current draft.

## Action Step #6: Your Key Scenes

Go through your list of scenes and identify your key scenes by placing an asterisk next to their name. You can add to this list later, as you expand your series; the point now is just to get started.

## Action Step #7: Name Your Series

Begin a list of your series by identifying the major movements that exist within your key scenes. Name each series just as you named each scene: with something you can remember that will bring you quickly back into the essence of that series.

## Action Step #8: Expand Your List of Series

Review the rest of your manuscript to expand your list of series until you have twelve to fifteen of them. Pay special attention to your "good" scenes for clues. Identify each iteration of a series by giving it an exponent.

## Action Step #9: Describe Your Series

Describe each of your series in one sentence that shows both its identity and the change that it undergoes. If a series does not undergo a change (if there is no appreciable variation within its repetition), notice that as well!

## Action Step #10: List Your Series Sentences

List your series sentences in a top-down order of importance.

## Action Step #11: Your One Thing

Distill your many series sentences into four, focusing on the largest series and their interactions. Continue to combine elements until this statement is two sentences, and then only one: This is your theme.

## Action Step #12: Accept Control

Examine your theme closely. Is it reflective of your beliefs? Is it entitled to your precious time and painstaking effort? Is it entitled to your reader's precious time and painstaking effort? How should it be altered to more closely align with the book you want (or need) to write?

## Action Step #13: Draw the Target

Draw a target and place your theme in the bull's-eye. Arrange each narrative element (scene, series, character, place) closer to or farther from the center based on its relevance to the theme.

## Action Step #14: Find the Outliers

Find the narrative elements that are the "outliers" on your target, either unrelated or only tangentially related to the others. If an element is tangential, you have some decisions to make about how important it could become. If an element is unrelated, you will need to either forge new connections or cut this material loose.

## Action Step #15: Your Central Series

Choose a series that reflects the basic timeline of your work, one that your reader can identify and track. You will use this central series first in each of the next three steps to learn tools that you can then apply to all of your other series.

## Action Step #16: Chronological Order vs. Narrative Order

Establish whether your central series will be presented in chronological order or narrative order. Make this decision for each of your major series. Remember: If your central series will be in narrative order, it may aid the reader to present many of your other series in chronological order.

## Action Step #17: Beginnings, Middles, and Ends

Examine the beginning, middle, and end of your central series to determine where you may be missing an iteration, or where you have iterations without effect. Then examine each of your major series in the same way, looking at the segments of their individual arcs.

## Action Step #18: Numbers of Iterations

Establish how many iterations will make up your central series and where the turning point(s) lie. Make this decision for each of your major series, assessing whether you need to have multiple ups and downs.

## Action Step #19: Order Your Key Scenes

Put your key scenes in the order in which you want to present your material. By now you have all of the necessary information to make this decision.

## Action Step #20: Order All of Your Scenes

Assign all of your scenes a number in the new order you will use going forward in your next draft. This is a big step, which paradoxically is best done quickly.

## Action Step #21: Fate of the Bad and Forgotten Scenes

Examine each bad and forgotten scene and decide whether it is worthy of your next draft. You may decide that you just cannot drag those scenes any further. Revision is a process by which things get combined, shortened, or expanded. It is also a process by which certain things get left out.

## Action Step #22: Restore Links and Segmentation

Each scene needs to be either linked to or segmented from the scene before it. Experiment with different kinds of links to create "scenic runs," or chapters. Once your chapters are established, you might title and/or number them to enhance their segmentation and create a clear road map for the reader.

# Reading Copy

## The Ugly Duckling

BY HANS CHRISTIAN ANDERSEN (1843)

*Translation by Mrs. Edgar Lucas (1910)*

The country was very lovely just then—it was summer. The wheat was golden and the oats still green. The hay was stacked in the rich low meadows, where the stork marched about on his long red legs, chattering in Egyptian, the language his mother had taught him.

Round about the field and meadow lay great woods, in the midst of which were deep lakes. Yes, the country certainly was lovely. In the sunniest spot stood an old mansion surrounded by a deep moat, and great dock leaves grew from the walls of the house right down to the water's edge. Some of them were so tall that a small child could stand upright under them. In among the leaves it was as secluded as in the depths of a forest, and there a duck was sitting on her nest. Her little ducklings were just about to be hatched, but she was quite tired of sitting, for it had lasted such a long time. Moreover, she had very few visitors, as the other ducks liked swimming about in the moat better than waddling up to sit under the dock leaves and gossip with her.

At last one egg after another began to crack. "Cheep, cheep!" they said. All the chicks had come to life and were poking their heads out.

"Quack, quack!" said the duck, and then they all quacked their hardest and looked about them on all sides among the green leaves. Their mother allowed them to look as much as they liked, for green is good for the eyes.

"How big the world is, to be sure!" said all the young ones. They certainly now had ever so much more room to move about than when they were inside their eggshells.

"Do you imagine this is the whole world?" said the mother. "It stretches a long way on the other side of the garden, right into the parson's field, though I have never been as far as that. I suppose you are all here now?" She got up and looked about. "No, I declare I have not got you all yet! The biggest egg is still there. How long is this going to take?" she said, and settled herself on the nest again.

"Well, how are you getting on?" said an old duck who had come to pay her a visit.

"This one egg is taking such a long time!" answered the sitting duck. "The shell will not crack. But now you must look at the others. They are the finest ducklings I have ever seen. They are all exactly like their father, the rascal!—yet he never comes to see me."

"Let me look at the egg which won't crack," said the old duck. "You may be sure that it is a turkey's egg! I was cheated like that once and I had no end of trouble and worry with the creatures, for I may tell you that they are afraid of the water. I simply could not get them into it. I quacked and snapped at them, but it all did no good. Let me see the egg! Yes, it is a turkey's egg. You just leave it alone, and teach the other children to swim."

"I will sit on it a little longer. I have sat so long already that I may as well go on till the Midsummer Fair comes round."

"Please yourself," said the old duck, and away she went.

At last the big egg cracked. "Cheep, cheep!" said the young one and tumbled out. How big and ugly he was! The duck looked at him.

"That is a monstrous big duckling," she said. "None of the others looked like that. Can he be a turkey chick? Well, we shall soon find that out. Into the water he shall go, if I have to kick him in myself."

Next day was gloriously fine, and the sun shone on all the green dock leaves. The mother duck with her whole family went down to the moat.

Splash! into the water she sprang. "Quack, quack," she said, and one duckling plumped in after the other. The water dashed over their heads, but they came up again and floated beautifully. Their legs went of themselves, and they were all there. Even the big ugly gray one swam about with them.

"No, that is no turkey," she said. "See how beautifully he

uses his legs and how erect he holds himself. He is my own chick, after all, and not bad looking when you come to look at him properly. Quack, quack! Now come with me and I will take you out into the world and introduce you to the duckyard. But keep close to me all the time so that no one will tread upon you. And beware of the cat!"

Then they went into the duckyard. There was a fearful uproar going on, for two broods were fighting for the head of an eel, and in the end the cat captured it.

"That's how things go in this world," said the mother duck, and she licked her bill, because she had wanted the eel's head herself.

"Now use your legs," said she. "Mind you quack properly, and bend your necks to the old duck over there. She is the grandest of us all. She has Spanish blood in her veins and that accounts for her size. And do you see? She has a red rag round her leg. That is a wonderfully fine thing, and the most extraordinary mark of distinction any duck can have. It shows clearly that she is not to be parted with, and that she is worthy of recognition both by beasts and men! Quack, now! Don't turn your toes in! A well brought-up duckling keeps his legs wide apart just like father and mother. That's it. Now bend your necks and say quack!"

They did as they were bid, but the other ducks round about looked at them and said, quite loud, "Just look there! Now we are to have that tribe, just as if there were not enough of us already. And, oh dear, how ugly that duckling is! We won't stand him." And a duck flew at him at once and bit him in the neck.

"Let him be," said the mother. "He is doing no harm."

"Very likely not," said the biter. "But he is so ungainly and queer that he must be whacked."

"Those are handsome children mother has," said the old duck with the rag round her leg. "They are all good looking except this one, but he is not a good specimen. It's a pity you can't make him over again."

"That can't be done, your grace," said the mother duck. "He is not handsome, but he is a thoroughly good creature, and he swims as beautifully as any of the others. I think I might venture even to add that I think he will improve as he goes on, or perhaps in time he may grow smaller. He was too long in the egg, and so he has not come out with a very good figure." And then she patted his neck and stroked him down. "Besides, he is a drake," said she. "So it does not matter so much. I believe he will be very strong, and I don't doubt at all that he will make his way in the world."

"The other ducklings are very pretty," said the old duck. "Now make yourselves quite at home, and if you find the head of an eel you may bring it to me."

After that they felt quite at home. But the poor duckling who had been the last to come out of the shell, and who was so ugly, was bitten, pushed about, and made fun of both by the ducks and the hens. "He is too big," they all said. And the turkey cock, who was born with his spurs on and therefore thought himself quite an emperor, puffed himself up like a vessel in full sail, made for him, and gobbled and gobbled till he became quite red in the face. The poor duckling did not know which way to turn. He was in despair because he was so ugly and the butt of the whole duckyard.

So the first day passed, and afterwards matters grew worse and worse. The poor duckling was chased and hustled by all of them. Even his brothers and sisters ill-used him. They were always saying, "If only the cat would get hold of you, you hideous object!" Even his mother said, "I wish to goodness you were miles away." The ducks bit him, the hens pecked him, and the girl who fed them kicked him aside.

Then he ran off and flew right over the hedge, where the little birds flew up into the air in a fright.

"That is because I am so ugly," thought the poor duckling, shutting his eyes, but he ran on all the same. Then he came to a great marsh where the wild ducks lived. He was so tired and miserable that he stayed there the whole night. In the morning the wild ducks flew up to inspect their new comrade.

"What sort of a creature are you?" they inquired, as the duckling turned from side to side and greeted them as well as he could. "You are frightfully ugly," said the wild ducks, "but that does not matter to us, so long as you do not marry into our family." Poor fellow! He had not thought of marriage. All he wanted was permission to lie among the rushes and to drink a little of the marsh water.

He stayed there two whole days. Then two wild geese came, or rather two wild ganders. They were not long out of the shell and therefore rather pert.

"I say, comrade," they said, "you are so ugly that we have taken quite a fancy to you! Will you join us and be a bird of passage? There is another marsh close by, and there are some charming wild geese there. All are sweet young ladies who can say quack! You are ugly enough to make your fortune among them."

Just at that moment, bang! bang! was heard up above, and both the wild geese fell dead among the reeds, and the water turned blood red. Bang! bang! went the guns, and flocks of wild geese flew from the rushes and the shots peppered among them again.

There was a grand shooting party, and the sportsmen lay hidden round the marsh. Some even sat on the branches of the trees which overhung the water. The blue smoke rose like clouds among the dark trees and swept over the pool.

The retrieving dogs wandered about in the swamp—splash! splash! The rushes and reeds bent beneath their tread on all sides. It was terribly alarming to the poor duckling. He twisted his head around to get it under his wing, and just at that moment a frightful big dog appeared close beside him. His tongue hung right out of his mouth and his eyes glared wickedly. He opened his great chasm of a mouth close to the duckling, showed his sharp teeth, and—splash!—went on without touching him.

"Oh, thank Heaven!" sighed the duckling. "I am so ugly that even the dog won't bite me!"

Then he lay quite still while the shots whistled among the bushes, and bang after bang rent the air. It only became quiet late in the day, but even then the poor duckling did not dare to get up. He waited several hours more before he looked about, and then he hurried away from the marsh as fast as he could. He ran across fields and meadows, and there was such a wind that he had hard work to make his way.

Towards night he reached a poor little cottage. It was such a miserable hovel that it could not make up its mind which way even to fall, and so it remained standing. The wind whistled so fiercely around the duckling that he had to sit on his tail to resist it, and it blew harder and ever harder. Then he saw that the door had fallen off one hinge and hung so crookedly that he could creep into the house through the crack, and so he made his way into the room.

An old woman lived here with her cat and her hen. The cat, whom she called "Sonnie," would arch his back, purr, and give off electric sparks if you stroked his fur the wrong way. The hen had quite tiny short legs, and so she was called "Chickie low legs." She laid good eggs, and the old woman was as fond of her as if she had been her own child.

In the morning the strange duckling was discovered immediately, and the cat began to purr and the hen to cluck.

"What on earth is that?" said the old woman, looking round, but her sight was not good and she thought the duckling was a fat duck which had escaped. "This is a wonderful find!" said she. "Now I shall have duck's eggs—if only it is not a drake. We must wait and see about that."

So she took the duckling on trial for three weeks, but no eggs made their appearance. The cat was master of this house and the hen its mistress. They always said, "We and the world," for they thought that they represented the half of the world, and that quite the better half.

The duckling thought there might be two opinions on the subject, but the hen would not hear of it.

"Can you lay eggs?" she asked.

"No."

"Have the goodness to hold your tongue then!"

And the cat said, "Can you arch your back, purr, or give off sparks?"

"No."

"Then you had better keep your opinions to yourself when people of sense are speaking!"

The duckling sat in the corner nursing his ill humor. Then he began to think of the fresh air and the sunshine, and an uncontrollable longing seized him to float on the water. At last he could not help telling the hen about it.

"What on earth possesses you?" she asked. "You have nothing to do. That is why you get these freaks into your head. Lay some eggs or take to purring, and you will get over it."

"But it is so delicious to float on the water," said the duckling. "It is so delicious to feel it rushing over your head when you dive to the bottom."

"That would be a fine amusement!" said the hen. "I think you have gone mad. Ask the cat about it. He is the wisest creature I know. Ask him if he is fond of floating on the water or diving under it. I say nothing about myself. Ask our mistress herself, the old woman. There is no one in the world cleverer than she is. Do you suppose she has any desire to float on the water or to duck underneath it?"

"You do not understand me," said the duckling.

"Well, if we don't understand you, who should? I suppose you don't consider yourself cleverer than the cat or the old woman, not to mention me! Don't make a fool of yourself, child, and thank your stars for all the good we have done you. Have you not lived in this warm room, and in such society that you might have learned something? But you are an idiot, and there is no pleasure in associating with you. You may believe me: I mean you well. I tell you home truths, and there is no surer way than that of knowing who are one's friends. You just set about laying some eggs, or learn to purr, or to emit sparks."

"I think I will go out into the wide world," said the duckling.

"Oh, do so by all means," said the hen.

So away went the duckling. He floated on the water and ducked underneath it, but he was looked at askance and was slighted by every living creature for his ugliness. Now autumn came. The leaves in the woods turned yellow and brown. The wind took hold of them, and they danced about. The sky looked very cold and the clouds hung heavy with snow and hail. A raven stood on the fence and croaked "Caw, caw!" from sheer cold. It made one shiver only to think of it. The poor duckling certainly was in a bad case!

One evening, the sun was just setting in wintry splendor when a flock of beautiful large birds appeared out of the bushes. The duckling had never seen anything so beautiful. They were dazzlingly white with long waving necks. They were swans, and uttering a peculiar cry they spread out their magnificent broad wings and flew away from the cold regions to warmer lands and open seas. They mounted so high, so very high, and the ugly little duckling became strangely uneasy. He circled round and round in the water like a wheel, craning his neck up into the air after them. Then he uttered a shriek so piercing and so strange that he was quite frightened by it himself. Oh, he could not forget those beautiful birds, those happy birds. And as soon as they were out of sight, he ducked right down to the bottom, and when he came up again he was quite beside himself. He did not know what the birds were, or whither they flew, but all the same he was more drawn towards them than he had ever been by any creatures before. He did not envy them in the least. How could it occur to him even to wish to be such a marvel of beauty? He would have been thankful if only the ducks would have tolerated him among them—the poor ugly creature.

The winter was so bitterly cold that the duckling was obliged to swim about in the water to keep it from freezing over, but every night the hole in which he swam got smaller and smaller. Then it froze so hard that the surface ice cracked, and the duckling had to use his legs all the time so that the ice should not freeze around him. At last he was so weary that he could move no more, and he was frozen fast into the ice.

Early in the morning a peasant came along and saw him. He went out onto the ice and hammered a hole in it with his heavy wooden shoe, and carried the duckling home to his wife. There he soon revived. The children wanted to play with him, but the duckling thought they were going to ill-use him, and rushed in his fright into the milk pan, and the milk spurted out all over the room. The woman shrieked and threw up her hands. Then he flew into the butter cask, and down into the meal tub and out again. Just imagine what he looked like by this time! The woman screamed and tried to hit him with the tongs. The children tumbled over one another in trying to catch him, and they screamed with laughter. By good luck the door stood open, and the duckling flew out among the bushes and the newly fallen snow. And he lay there thoroughly exhausted.

But it would be too sad to mention all the privation and misery he had to go through during the hard winter. When the sun began to shine warmly again, the duckling was in the marsh, lying among the rushes. The larks were singing and the beautiful spring had come.

Then all at once he raised his wings and they flapped with much greater strength than before and bore him off vigorously. Before he knew where he was, he found himself in a large garden where the apple trees were in full blossom and the air was scented with lilacs, the long branches of which overhung the indented shores of the lake. Oh, the spring freshness was delicious!

Just in front of him he saw three beautiful white swans advancing towards him from a thicket. With rustling feathers they swam lightly over the water. The duckling recognized the majestic birds, and he was overcome by a strange melancholy.

"I will fly to them, the royal birds, and they will hack me to pieces because I, who am so ugly, venture to approach them. But it won't matter! Better be killed by them than be snapped at by the ducks, pecked by the hens, spurned by the henwife, or suffer so much misery in the winter."

So he flew into the water and swam towards the stately swans. They saw him and darted towards him with ruffled feathers.

"Kill me!" said the poor creature, and he bowed his head towards the water and awaited his death. But what did he see reflected in the transparent water?

He saw below him his own image, but he was no longer a clumsy dark gray bird, ugly and ungainly. He was himself a swan! It does not matter in the least having been born in a duck-yard, if only you come out of a swan's egg!

He felt quite glad of all the misery and tribulation he had

gone through, for he was the better able to appreciate his good fortune now and all the beauty which greeted him. The big swans swam round and round him and stroked him with their bills.

Some little children came into the garden with corn and pieces of bread which they threw into the water, and the smallest one cried out, "There is a new one!" The other children shouted with joy, "Yes, a new one has come." And they clapped their hands and danced about, running after their father and mother. They threw the bread into the water, and one and all said, "The new one is the prettiest of them all. He is so young and handsome." And the old swans bent their heads and did homage before him.

He felt quite shy, and hid his head under his wing. He did not know what to think. He was very happy, but not at all proud, for a good heart never becomes proud. He thought of how he had been pursued and scorned, and now he heard them all say that he was the most beautiful of all beautiful birds. The lilacs bent their boughs right down into the water before him, and the bright sun was warm and cheering. He rustled his feathers and raised his slender neck aloft, saying with exultation in his heart, "I never dreamt of so much happiness when I was the Ugly Duckling!"

# Annotated Copy

The <u>Ugly</u>[1] Duckling[1]

## Key

| bold line | ———————— | scene separation |
|---|---|---|
| dotted line | – – – – – – – – | alternate scene separation |
| small capitals text | WEATHER[1] | weather series |
| underlined text | <u>UGLINESS</u>[1] | ugliness series |
| bolded text | **PAIN/AGGRESSION**[1] | pain/aggression series |
| italicized text | *Identity*[1] | identity series |
| capitalized, bolded text | **THEME** | one-sentence statement |

*(begin scene one)*

THE COUNTRY WAS VERY LOVELY JUST THEN—IT WAS SUMMER.[1] The wheat was golden and the oats still green. The hay was stacked in the rich low meadows, where the stork marched about on his long red legs, chattering in Egyptian, the language his mother had taught him.

Round about the field and meadow lay great woods, in the midst of which were deep lakes. Yes, the country certainly was lovely. In the sunniest spot stood an old mansion surrounded by a deep moat, and great dock leaves grew from the walls of the house right down to the water's edge. Some of them were so tall that a small child could stand upright under them. In among the leaves it was as secluded as in the depths of a forest, and there a duck was sitting on her nest. *Her little ducklings were just about to be hatched, but she was quite tired of sitting, for it had lasted such a long time.*[2] Moreover, she had very few visitors, as the other ducks liked swimming about in the moat better than waddling up to sit under the dock leaves and gossip with her.

At last one egg after another began to crack. "Cheep, cheep!" they said. All the chicks had come to life and were poking their heads out.

"Quack, quack!" said the duck, and then they all quacked their hardest and looked about them on all sides among the green leaves. Their mother allowed them to look as much as they liked, for green is good for the eyes.

"How big the world is, to be sure!" said all the young ones. They certainly now had ever so much more room to move about than when they were inside their eggshells.

"Do you imagine this is the whole world?" said the mother. "It stretches a long way on the other side of the garden, right into the parson's field, though I have never been as far as that. I suppose you are all here now?" She got up and looked about. "No, I declare I have not got you all yet! The biggest egg is still there. How long is this going to take?" she said, and settled herself on the nest again.

"Well, how are you getting on?" said an old duck who had come to pay her a visit.

"This one egg is taking such a long time!" answered the sitting duck. "The shell will not crack. But now you must look at the others. They are the finest ducklings I have ever seen. They are all exactly like their father, the rascal!—yet he never comes to see me."

*"Let me look at the egg which won't crack," said the old duck. "You may be sure that it is a turkey's egg!*[3] I was cheated like that once and I had no end of trouble and worry with the creatures, for I may tell you that they are afraid of the water. I simply could not get them into it. I quacked and snapped at them, but it all did no good. Let me see the egg! Yes, it is a turkey's egg. You just leave it alone, and teach the other children to swim."

"I will sit on it a little longer. I have sat so long already that I may as well go on till the Midsummer Fair comes round."

"Please yourself," said the old duck, and away she went.

At last the big egg cracked. "Cheep, cheep!" said the young one and tumbled out. <u>How big and ugly he was! The duck looked at him.</u>

<u>"That is a monstrous big duckling,"</u>[2] she said. "None of the others looked like that. Can he be a turkey chick? **Well, we shall**

**soon find that out. Into the water he shall go, if I have to kick him in myself."**[1]

*(end scene one)*

---

*(begin scene two)*

NEXT DAY WAS GLORIOUSLY FINE, AND THE SUN SHONE ON ALL THE GREEN DOCK LEAVES.[2] The mother duck with her whole family went down to the moat.

Splash! into the water she sprang. "Quack, quack," she said, and one duckling plumped in after the other. The water dashed over their heads, but they came up again and floated beautifully. Their legs went of themselves, and they were all there. <u>Even the big ugly gray one swam about with them.</u>[3]

*"No, that is no turkey," she said. "See how beautifully he uses his legs and how erect he holds himself. He is my own chick, after all,*[4] and not bad looking when you come to look at him properly. Quack, quack! Now come with me and I will take you out into the world and introduce you to the duckyard. But keep close to me all the time so that no one will tread upon you. And beware of the cat!"

Then they went into the duckyard. There was a fearful uproar going on, for two broods were fighting for the head of an eel, and in the end the cat captured it.

"That's how things go in this world," said the mother duck, and she licked her bill, because she had wanted the eel's head herself.

"Now use your legs," said she. "Mind you quack properly,

and bend your necks to the old duck over there. She is the grand-est of us all. She has Spanish blood in her veins and that ac-counts for her size. And do you see? She has a red rag round her leg. That is a wonderfully fine thing, and the most extraordinary mark of distinction any duck can have. It shows clearly that she is not to be parted with, and that she is worthy of recognition both by beasts and men! Quack, now! Don't turn your toes in! A well brought-up duckling keeps his legs wide apart just like fa-ther and mother. That's it. Now bend your necks and say quack!"

They did as they were bid, but the other ducks round about looked at them and said, quite loud, "Just look there! Now we are to have that tribe, just as if there were not enough of us al-ready. <u>And, oh dear, how ugly that duckling is!</u>[4] **We won't stand him." And a duck flew at him at once and bit him in the neck.**[2]

"Let him be," said the mother. "He is doing no harm."

"Very likely not," said the biter. "But he is so ungainly and queer that he must be whacked."

"Those are handsome children mother has," said the old duck with the rag round her leg. "They are all good looking ex-cept this one, but he is not a good specimen. It's a pity you can't make him over again."

"That can't be done, your grace," said the mother duck. "He is not handsome, but he is a thoroughly good creature, and he swims as beautifully as any of the others. I think I might venture even to add that I think he will improve as he goes on, or per-haps in time he may grow smaller. He was too long in the egg, and so he has not come out with a very good figure." And then she patted his neck and stroked him down. "Besides, he is a drake," said she. "So it does not matter so much. I believe he will be very strong, and I don't doubt at all that he will make his way in the world."

"The other ducklings are very pretty," said the old duck. "Now make yourselves quite at home, and if you find the head of an eel you may bring it to me."

After that they felt quite at home. <u>But the poor duckling who had been the last to come out of the shell, and who was so ugly,</u>[5] **was bitten, pushed about, and made fun of both by the ducks and the hens.**[3] "He is too big," they all said. And the turkey cock, who was born with his spurs on and therefore thought himself quite an emperor, puffed himself up like a vessel in full sail, made for him, and gobbled and gobbled till he became quite red in the face. The poor duckling did not know which way to turn. <u>He was in despair because he was so ugly</u>[6] and the butt of the whole duckyard.

*(end scene two)*

---

*(begin scene three)*

So the first day passed, and afterwards matters grew worse and worse. The poor duckling was chased and hustled by all of them. Even his brothers and sisters ill-used him. They were always saying, <u>"If only the cat would get hold of you, you hideous object!"</u>[7] Even his mother said, "I wish to goodness you were miles away." **The ducks bit him, the hens pecked him, and the girl who fed them kicked him aside.**[4]

Then he ran off and flew right over the hedge, where the little birds flew up into the air in a fright.

"That is because I am so ugly," thought the poor duckling, shutting his eyes, but he ran on all the same. Then he came to a great marsh where the wild ducks lived. He was so tired and miserable that he stayed there the whole night. In the morning the wild ducks flew up to inspect their new comrade.

*"What sort of a creature are you?" they inquired, as the duckling turned from side to side and greeted them as well as he could.*[5] "You are frightfully ugly," said the wild ducks, "but that does not matter to us, so long as you do not marry into our family."[8] Poor fellow! He had not thought of marriage. All he wanted was permission to lie among the rushes and to drink a little of the marsh water.

He stayed there two whole days. Then two wild geese came, or rather two wild ganders. They were not long out of the shell and therefore rather pert.

"I say, comrade," they said, "you are so ugly that we have taken quite a fancy to you!"[9] Will you join us and be a bird of passage? There is another marsh close by, and there are some charming wild geese there. All are sweet young ladies who can say quack! You are ugly enough to make your fortune among them." Just at that moment, bang! bang! was heard up above, and both the wild geese fell dead among the reeds, and the water turned blood red. Bang! bang! went the guns, and flocks of wild geese flew from the rushes and the shots peppered among them again.

There was a grand shooting party, and the sportsmen lay hidden round the marsh. Some even sat on the branches of the trees which overhung the water. The blue smoke rose like clouds among the dark trees and swept over the pool.

The retrieving dogs wandered about in the swamp—splash! splash! The rushes and reeds bent beneath their tread on all sides. It was terribly alarming to the poor duckling. He twisted his head around to get it under his wing, and just at that moment a frightful big dog appeared close beside him. His tongue hung right out of his mouth and his eyes glared wickedly. He opened his great chasm of a mouth close to the duckling, showed his sharp teeth, and—splash!—went on without touching him.

<u>"Oh, thank Heaven!" sighed the duckling. "I am so ugly that even the dog won't bite me!"</u>[10]

Then he lay quite still while the shots whistled among the bushes, and bang after bang rent the air. It only became quiet late in the day, but even then the poor duckling did not dare to get up. He waited several hours more before he looked about, and then he hurried away from the marsh as fast as he could. He ran across fields and meadows, and there was such a wind that he had hard work to make his way.

*(end scene three)*

---

*(begin scene four)*

Towards night he reached a poor little cottage. It was such a miserable hovel that it could not make up its mind which way even to fall, and so it remained standing. THE WIND WHISTLED SO FIERCELY AROUND THE DUCKLING THAT HE HAD TO SIT ON HIS

TAIL TO RESIST IT, AND IT BLEW HARDER AND EVER HARDER.[3] Then he saw that the door had fallen off one hinge and hung so crookedly that he could creep into the house through the crack, and so he made his way into the room.

An old woman lived here with her cat and her hen. The cat, whom she called "Sonnie," would arch his back, purr, and give off electric sparks if you stroked his fur the wrong way. The hen had quite tiny short legs, and so she was called "Chickie low legs." She laid good eggs, and the old woman was as fond of her as if she had been her own child.

In the morning the strange duckling was discovered immediately, and the cat began to purr and the hen to cluck.

*"What on earth is that?" said the old woman, looking round, but her sight was not good and she thought the duckling was a fat duck which had escaped.*[6] "This is a wonderful find!" said she. "Now I shall have duck's eggs—if only it is not a drake. We must wait and see about that."

So she took the duckling on trial for three weeks, but no eggs made their appearance. The cat was master of this house and the hen its mistress. They always said, "We and the world," for they thought that they represented the half of the world, and that quite the better half.

The duckling thought there might be two opinions on the subject, but the hen would not hear of it.

"Can you lay eggs?" she asked.

"No."

"Have the goodness to hold your tongue then!"

And the cat said, "Can you arch your back, purr, or give off sparks?"

"No."

"Then you had better keep your opinions to yourself when people of sense are speaking!"

The duckling sat in the corner nursing his ill humor. Then he began to think of the fresh air and the sunshine, and an uncontrollable longing seized him to float on the water. At last he could not help telling the hen about it.

"What on earth possesses you?" she asked. "You have nothing to do. That is why you get these freaks into your head. Lay some eggs or take to purring, and you will get over it."

"But it is so delicious to float on the water," said the duckling. "It is so delicious to feel it rushing over your head when you dive to the bottom."

"That would be a fine amusement!" said the hen. "I think you have gone mad. Ask the cat about it. He is the wisest creature I know. Ask him if he is fond of floating on the water or diving under it. I say nothing about myself. Ask our mistress herself, the old woman. There is no one in the world cleverer than she is. Do you suppose she has any desire to float on the water or to duck underneath it?"

"You do not understand me," said the duckling.

"Well, if we don't understand you, who should? I suppose you don't consider yourself cleverer than the cat or the old woman, not to mention me! Don't make a fool of yourself, child, and thank your stars for all the good we have done you. Have you not lived in this warm room, and in such society that you might have learned something? But you are an idiot, and there is no pleasure in associating with you. You may believe me: I mean you well. I tell you home truths, and there is no surer way than that of knowing who are one's friends. You just set about laying some eggs, or learn to purr, or to emit sparks."

"I think I will go out into the wide world," said the duckling.

"Oh, do so by all means," said the hen.

*(end scene four)*

---

*(begin scene five)*

So away went the duckling. He floated on the water and ducked underneath it, <u>but he was looked at askance and was slighted by every living creature for his ugliness.</u>[11] Now AU-TUMN CAME. THE LEAVES IN THE WOODS TURNED YELLOW AND BROWN. THE WIND TOOK HOLD OF THEM, AND THEY DANCED ABOUT. THE SKY LOOKED VERY COLD AND THE CLOUDS HUNG HEAVY WITH SNOW AND HAIL. A RAVEN STOOD ON THE FENCE AND CROAKED "CAW, CAW!" FROM SHEER COLD. IT MADE ONE SHIVER ONLY TO THINK OF IT.[4] The poor duckling certainly was in a bad case!

*(alternate end scene four)*

- - - - - - - - - - - - - - - - - - - - - - - - - - - - - - - - - - - - - - - - - - - - -

*(alternate begin scene five)*

One evening, the sun was just setting in wintry splendor when *a flock of beautiful large birds appeared out of the bushes. The duckling had never seen anything so beautiful. They were dazzlingly white with long waving necks. They were swans,*[7] and uttering a peculiar cry they spread out their magnificent broad wings and flew away from the cold regions to warmer lands and open seas. They mounted so high, so very high, and the ugly little duckling became strangely uneasy. He circled round and round in the water like a wheel, craning his neck up into the air after them. Then he uttered a shriek so piercing and so strange that he was quite frightened by it himself. Oh, he could not forget those beautiful birds, those happy birds. And as soon as they were out of sight, he ducked right down to the bottom, and when he came up again he was quite beside himself. *He did not know what the birds were, or whither they flew, but all the same he was more drawn towards them than he had ever been by any creatures before.*[8] He did not envy them in the least. How could it occur to him even to wish to be such a marvel of beauty? He would have been thankful if only the ducks would have tolerated him among them—the poor ugly creature.[12]

THE WINTER WAS SO BITTERLY COLD THAT THE DUCKLING WAS OBLIGED TO SWIM ABOUT IN THE WATER TO KEEP IT FROM FREEZING OVER, BUT EVERY NIGHT THE HOLE IN WHICH HE SWAM GOT SMALLER AND SMALLER.[5] Then it froze so hard that the surface ice cracked, and the duckling had to use his legs all the time so that the ice should not freeze around him. At last he was so weary that he could move no more, and he was frozen fast into the ice.

Early in the morning a peasant came along and saw him. He went out onto the ice and hammered a hole in it with his heavy wooden shoe, and carried the duckling home to his wife. There he soon revived. **The children wanted to play with him, but**

**the duckling thought they were going to ill-use him, and rushed in his fright into the milk pan, and the milk spurted out all over the room.**[5] The woman shrieked and threw up her hands. Then he flew into the butter cask, and down into the meal tub and out again. Just imagine what he looked like by this time! The woman screamed and tried to hit him with the tongs. The children tumbled over one another in trying to catch him, and they screamed with laughter. By good luck the door stood open, and the duckling flew out among the bushes and the newly fallen snow. And he lay there thoroughly exhausted.

BUT IT WOULD BE TOO SAD TO MENTION ALL THE PRIVATION AND MISERY HE HAD TO GO THROUGH DURING THE HARD WINTER. WHEN THE SUN BEGAN TO SHINE WARMLY AGAIN, THE DUCKLING WAS IN THE MARSH, LYING AMONG THE RUSHES. THE LARKS WERE SINGING AND THE BEAUTIFUL SPRING HAD COME.[6]

*(end scene five)*

---

*(begin scene six)*

Then all at once he raised his wings and they flapped with much greater strength than before and bore him off vigorously. Before he knew where he was, he found himself in a large garden where the apple trees were in full blossom and the air was scented with lilacs, the long branches of which overhung the indented shores of the lake. OH, THE SPRING FRESHNESS WAS DELICIOUS![7]

Just in front of him he saw three beautiful white swans advancing towards him from a thicket. With rustling feathers they swam lightly over the water. The duckling recognized the majestic birds, and he was overcome by a strange melancholy.

*"I will fly to them, the royal birds,*[9] **and they will hack me to pieces because** I, who am so ugly, venture to approach them.[13] But it won't matter! **Better be killed by them than be snapped at by the ducks, pecked by the hens, spurned by the hen-wife,**[6] or suffer SO MUCH MISERY IN THE WINTER."[8]

So he flew into the water and swam towards the stately swans. They saw him and darted towards him with ruffled feathers.

"Kill me!" said the poor creature, and he bowed his head towards the water and awaited his death. But what did he see reflected in the transparent water?

*He saw below him his own image, but he was no longer* a clumsy *dark gray bird,* ugly and ungainly.[14] *He was himself a swan!*[10] **IT DOES NOT MATTER IN THE LEAST HAVING BEEN BORN IN A DUCKYARD, IF ONLY YOU COME OUT OF A SWAN'S EGG!**

He felt quite glad of all the misery and tribulation he had gone through, for he was the better able to appreciate his good fortune now and all the beauty which greeted him. The big swans swam round and round him and **stroked him with their bills.**[7]

Some little children came into the garden with corn and pieces of bread which they threw into the water, and the smallest one cried out, "There is a new one!" The other children shouted with joy, *"Yes, a new one has come."*[11] And they clapped their hands and danced about, running after their father and mother. They threw the bread into the water, and one and all said, "The new one is the prettiest of them all. He is so young and handsome.[15]" And the old swans bent their heads and did homage before him.

He felt quite shy, and hid his head under his wing. He did not know what to think. He was very happy, but not at all proud, for a good heart never becomes proud. He thought of how he had been pursued and scorned, and now he heard them all say that he was the most beautiful of all beautiful birds. The lilacs bent their boughs right down into the water before him, and the BRIGHT SUN WAS WARM AND CHEERING.[9] He rustled his feathers and raised his slender neck aloft, saying with exultation in his heart, "I never dreamt of so much happiness *when I was the Ugly Duckling!*"[12]

# Guide for Beta Readers

## Using the Book Architecture Method in Workshops and/or with Well-Intentioned Individual Readers

There comes a time when every writer wants feedback. The problem is that no one knows exactly how to give feedback (receiving feedback is another story, which we will touch on shortly). It's not the fault of our beta readers that our request for feedback is so amorphous.* They are just trying to help us, and we need to give them the tools. One of the strong points of this method, I think, is that it gives us a format with which to solicit targeted responses.

As I mentioned in "How to Generate Material" at the beginning of this book, it is important to find a neutral audience to write for. Neither extreme of the critic or the cheerleader will really help us get better. In class I have only one rule: You can't

---

* *Beta readers* is the term applied to individuals who read your work before it is finished. Why they aren't called alpha readers? I don't know—maybe that's you?

say about someone else's work that you loved it, and you can't say, "I think I'm really just not your audience" (i.e., I hated it). Being a beta reader is a serious responsibility that requires you to "check your ego at the door."* If beta readers really can put aside their feelings for what your work brings up for them personally—if they can own their projections, in other words—then together you can look deeply into the work before you.

The first question we ask our beta readers (and this will come to you as no surprise, I'm sure) is:

What scenes do you remember from the book you just read?

Not every beta reader will have a working definition of scene, so while you can offer the five definitions provided in this book (a scene is where something happens, is where something changes, is related to the theme of the work, is capable of series, and has "it"), it is also instructive to see what people think is a scene. In class we will list on a blackboard dozens of events, conversations, character realizations, any memorable scrap of the work in question. As we saw in Chapter Six, it is also noteworthy what no one mentions. When your group of beta readers collectively forget your favorite scene, it might time to kill a darling.

The next questions have to be carefully couched given the way we are navigating between critic and cheerleader. After supplying some criteria for "good" and "bad" scenes, we ask:

---

* As producer Quincy Jones told the music superstars upon their arrival at the taping of the song "We Are the World."

Which of these scenes are good? Which of these scenes
are bad?

You hope to receive a fairly equal balance between good and
bad scenes from your beta reader. There is work to be done,
clearly, but not all hope is lost. Besides, now we have a method
for working with the bad, for retaining the good, and for developing the missed opportunities that exist in the manuscript in
its current form.

Next we ask our beta readers:

Which of these scenes are the key scenes?

It is possible to get everyone up to speed on key scenes as the
bridge between scene and series in Action Step #6. But it is also
possible simply to ask, "Where did you feel there was an emotional payoff?" "Of the good scenes, which were the most memorable?" "Where was there a point of no return, where profound
changes or major consequences occurred?"

At that point in class we take a picture of the blackboard
with a smartphone and then we erase everything but the key
scenes. Watching 80 percent of our jottings disappear can be a
magical moment; the essence of the book begins to show itself in
bold relief. If you are working with an individual beta reader not
in a classroom setting, this is when interacting with him or her,
virtually or in person, can be useful. You can meet your beta
reader for coffee, or beer, and exchange ideas in a more rapid
brainstorming session.

With just a few scenes placed randomly on the blackboard now, we circle each in turn and ask:

What series are present in these scenes?

The question is twofold: While we name individual series in a writer's work, we also naturally discuss the way these series interact—such is the nature of key scenes. Arrows can be drawn between two key scenes indicating how the series goes up or down, through its process of improvement and deterioration. Sometimes these arrows intersect with other key scenes. Sometimes in the middle of these crisscrossing lines a center emerges that looks like . . . you guessed it . . . a theme.

What is the central theme of this work? What is the one thing that this work is about?

Early on in the method, I suggested that you, the author, write down what you thought your own theme was, before doing all of the excavation that hopefully leads to great insight. (This was before we realized that your book both is and is not about this initial theme—what you set out to do is something like what you did . . . but not exactly.)

A writer reads his or her initial four-line thematic statement aloud, and then we check with our beta readers to see if that's what they think the book is about. At this point, things can get a little dicey. Writers can get a little proprietary about what they think is theirs. It isn't theirs, of course; the act of writing is an act of communication that, once made, belongs to all of us—but this realization comes gradually.

At this point, writers should be reminded that, hey—it's your book. What you need to do right now is take it in, all of it: the good scenes and the bad scenes, the off-base remarks and the right-on-target remarks—just listen. Later you can sort out what makes sense to you; in fact, it will sort itself out for you. And if you need to, you can stand up for what you believe about a specific scene, how that part needs to go. But you don't need to do it now. Writers really do have to be told these things. Personally, I can't hear it enough.

In class, we negotiate a theme that most students, including the writer, can live with. The blackboard is then erased completely, and only the theme is written in the center. At this point it is helpful for someone to read off all of the scenes from the picture we took with a smartphone earlier.

> With each given scene, how close to or far from the theme does it belong?

This is where discussion can include some of the material offered in traditional workshops. Do we feel like this character is alive, able to make unusual choices and mistakes, or does it feel like a derivation of someone the writer knows? Where do we feel like the authorial voice is overbearing, and where do we feel like the narration is a delight to follow along with? (It doesn't all have to be method, you know . . .)

Hopefully what follows at this point is that the writer

experiences a sense of relief. He or she sees where the heart of the book lies, instead of just having the vague sense that something was wrong with it. That string of scenes that you thought was a tangent was a tangent—it didn't even make the circles of the archery target. That whole part you didn't want to write doesn't have to be written. What's better than that?

We're not actually going to rewrite the book in class, but we can offer a little more insight before the proverbial bell rings:

What is the central series of the work?

Or, what does the central series appear to be at this juncture? These are works in progress, yet we can still ask: What is keeping time? Which series grounds us the most in what is actually going on, what is at stake? Should that series be presented in straight chronological order, or would presenting events in a narrative order work to greater effect? Is the central series—or any other series we have been able to identify, for that matter—missing something? A beginning, a middle, or an end, perhaps?

When a writer and beta reader work together most productively, it is as if they get away from the notion of "constructive feedback" all together and engage in what we might call "reconstructive feedback." Responses contribute powerful information to a writer's creative process. Organization and revision will require the same effort as before (or more), but those efforts will be greatly streamlined and more effective.

# Glossary of Terms

## Related to the Book Architecture Method

**Bad Scenes** Bad scenes are scenes that don't "work." Sometimes they are just uninteresting; sometimes they are unrelated to your theme. Bad scenes can provoke anxiety before they are rewritten because they bear a message about your book—they cannot simply be jettisoned, although that is a possibility in the end. A bad scene is like a bad relationship: you have to find out what is bad about it, or else you risk repeating it.

**Catharsis** People read books because they want to believe they can change. This change takes place, as Aristotle noted, when a narrative arouses "pity" and "fear" in a reader. We go from the sense that we are fine (even though we aren't, really) to experiencing anxiety; when we are "purged" of these emotions, we emerge a percentage more alive. Catharsis thus makes room for scenes that create discomfort, confusion, or some sense of threat, as well as scenes that provide resolution and understanding.

**Central Series** A central series orients your reader to the direction of the work and to where the overall emotion and tension go up or down. The central series is also known as the *timekeeper series* because it allows the reader to know what day (or year) it is. The central series grounds the reader in what is going on—what is at stake, what the question is—in its simplest terms.

**Change** *See* IDENTITY/CHANGE.

**Chronological Order** *See* NARRATIVE ORDER/CHRONOLOGICAL ORDER.

**Flashback** A flashback occurs when you leave the present timeline to recount something that happened previously. There are four guidelines to keep in mind when using a flashback: (1) Use a flashback for a reason, which is revealed to the reader. (2) Don't leave the present time period for so long that readers lose their bearings upon return. (3) Don't flash back for too short a time (such as a few lines or a paragraph, which you can give us as a memory in the present). (4) A flashback should still be presented in *scene*, with all of the benefits a scene creates: immediacy, reality, and suspense. (*See* NARRATIVE ORDER/CHRONOLOGICAL ORDER.)

**Foreshadowing** Foreshadowing denotes an *iteration* that occurs early in a *series*. Foreshadowing therefore establishes the existence of a series in the narrative, but in an indirect way that merely plants a seed in the reader's mind. Effective foreshadowing inspires curiosity without either excess clarity or confusion (unless this confusion is intended, as in the "red herring").

**Forgotten Scenes** A forgotten scene is one you were not able to recollect when you brainstormed your list of scenes in Action Step #1. Forgetting a scene doesn't mean you have to take it out; a forgotten scene can be profitably combined with another scene, or it might be a placeholder for material that you will later develop, or it is fine—you just forgot it. The fact that it was forgotten is strike one, not strike three. But it is strike one and should be considered as such.

**Good Scenes** Good scenes are scenes that "work." During the act of revision, we leave the good scenes pretty much alone. Therefore the question "Is it good?" in the context of using this method is really "Is it good enough?" Good enough that you don't have to do anything about it right now? Good enough that if you had to show someone one of your scenes, you would be okay with their seeing this one?

**Identity** *See* IDENTITY/CHANGE.

**Identity/Change** Identity is to change as repetition is to variation. Writers often find it more helpful to use the terms *identity* and *change* when they analyze their characters in the context of series. Identity refers to the static quality of a character that repeats from day to day (dialect, costume, outlook, relationships, etc.) and makes it possible to "identify" a character. A well-drawn character has his or her identity firmly established, thus earning either the praise of being "consistent" or the criticism that he or she has acted "out of character."

Knowing what to expect from a character sets up his or her change. Forster classified characters as either *round* or *flat* depending on how much change they go through. A round character might go through a change of heart so transformative that the reader undergoes a change along with him or her—the empathic experience known as *catharsis*. On the other end of the spectrum are the characters who don't change: either the stock or flat character who fulfills one specific purpose only, or the character we forgot to change, which our *series* work can help us identify.

**In Medias Res** Writers are often advised to begin *in medias res*. The mistranslation of this term as "in the middle" has given birth to several novels in which the narrative begins with a scene that belongs to the middle of the book; we then pull back and get every other scene in *chronological order*. (*See* NARRATIVE ORDER/ CHRONOLOGICAL ORDER.) *In medias res* actually means "into the middle of things"; we still begin at the beginning but we choose an inciting incident where exposition can be provided at the same time as the "springs of the action."

**Iteration** Each item in a *series* is referred to as an iteration. By definition, there can never be one iteration of a series; to create a series is to provide the reader with iterations that both repeat a subject and vary it. *Iteration* is related to the word *reiterated*. To reiterate something is to repeat it, any number of times, for emphasis. Nothing is ever the same the second time, however, because the context has changed—thus repetition gives birth to variation, and the interplay between repetition and variation forms the core of the concept of series.

**Key Scene** A key scene is a scene in which multiple series intersect. In a key scene, the reader gets the feeling that "it is all coming together." A key scene is rarely located in the beginning of a text, as the individual series that will interact have not yet been sufficiently established. A key scene is where the reader's expectations are (at least partially) satisfied, where there is an emotional payoff. Key scenes may amount to approximately 15 percent of your scenes and be near the top of the list of scenes you brainstormed originally.

**Limitation** Limitation is the key to revision. Pretty much anything can be limited: the number of scenes, series, characters, locations, points of view, plot twists and turns, and time-jumps (*flashbacks* and *flash-forwards*). People do not like to be limited in general, but limitation serves the goal of *unity* in a unique and irreplaceable way. Nothing limits your material better than a good *theme*.

**Links** Links are passages, from a single phrase to several pages in length, that join two scenes together. Links can be seamless, smooth, and unobtrusive, and contribute to a reader's "willing suspension of disbelief." Links can also be ornamental, and draw attention to themselves through an extroverted use of voice. Links establish logic, creating a succession between scenes that amounts to a causal connection. A weak link will cause your reader's attention to wander, or, worse, snap. (*See* WHITE SPACE.)

**Missing Scenes** A missing scene is either a scene you have had in mind to write but haven't yet or a scene you have discovered the need for by finding a hole in your material. Missing scenes can show how your narrative wants to evolve and where the heart of your book truly lies. Any time you want to write a missing scene, you should put this book down and write it—it will give you some answers to the questions this method keeps asking.

**Narrative Arc** In a *series* that is working, iterations are presented in an order that communicates direction. This evolution might be a process of deterioration or improvement, or a combination, and the overall movement of an individual series is what is known as the narrative arc. There is never just one narrative arc in a book-length work; rather, each series has its own narrative arc. Constructing or creating an individual narrative arc is much easier to accomplish when the iterations of that series are charted. The terms *character arc* and *narrative arc* can be used interchangeably; each round character has his or her own arc. (*See* IDENTITY/ CHANGE.)

**Narrative Order** *See* NARRATIVE ORDER/CHRONOLOGICAL ORDER.

**Narrative Order/Chronological Order** Both narrative order and chronological order refer to the way in which events are presented to the reader. In chronological order, events are reported chronologically; the order in which they happened is the order in which the reader receives them. With narrative order, however, these events are rearranged for dramatic or psychological effect. Narrative order makes use of techniques such as *flashback*; both narrative and chronological order can benefit from techniques such as *foreshadowing*.

**Outliers** Outliers are narrative elements that are either unrelated or only tangentially related to your theme. They get their name from appearing on the periphery of your target in Action Step #14. If an element is unrelated to the theme, you will need to forge new connections or cut the material loose. If it is tangential to your theme, you need to decide how important it could become.

**Repetition** *See* REPETITION/VARIATION.

**Repetition/Variation** A *series* is formed by the repetition of a narrative element (such as a person, an object, a phrase, or a place) in such a way that it undergoes a clear evolution. These repetitions—with their attendant variations—may exist in different scenes, or they may exist in the same scene, or both. Over the course of a book-length manuscript, the repetition and variation of narrative elements is what produces meaning. Repetition without variation can build the internal pressure of the story, leading the reader to seek some narrative resolution. Once repetitions have been clearly established, variations will have an even more powerful impact on the reader. When discussing characters, we might substitute *identity* for repetition and *change* for variation.

**Scene** Scenes are the building blocks of your work. Discovering these individual, relatively self-contained narrative passages creates the foundation for your revision; you can now move scenes around, divide and combine them, and eliminate them when necessary. A scene is where something happens, and because something happens, something changes in a way that propels the narrative. Additionally, a scene must be related to the central *theme* of the book and be capable of *series*. Finally, a scene must have "it"—it must carry with it a sense of excitement, for both the writer and the reader.

**Segmentation** Segmentation refers to the way in which a narrative is divided: for example, book chapters, theatrical acts, miniseries episodes. Within a given chapter, certain scenes are fused via *links*; when that group of scenes or chapter is separated from another group of scenes, we have segmentation. Segmentation benefits our attention span by allowing us time to let part of the narrative sink in before we need to absorb new information.

**Series** Anything that repeats and varies in your work can be considered a series (each occurrence or example of that series is called an *iteration*). These repetitions and variations of a series can be traced as they develop, creating a sense of direction known as the *narrative arc*. For the purposes of this method, it is best to track only twelve to fifteen series for a book-length work. You might focus on major elements such as a person (characters can be series); a relationship that has an up and a down; an object, which becomes a symbol through series; or a saying, which can become the work's *theme*. Series can be conceptual, but an abstract series may include too many things and be too difficult to track through all of its iterations. Remember, a complex book does not come from complex series that are difficult to navigate; complexity comes from clear, meaningful series that intersect and interact in unusual and consequential ways.

**Theme** Your theme is the central conflict or concept of your work, its thesis. Your theme is the one thing that your book is about (because your book can only be about one thing). At times a condensed, one-sentence theme may look like a cliché, but bear in mind that the value a theme has for informing the organization and revision of your material does not come from its originality—it comes from being about one thing. You may have heard about the themes (plural) that a good book has; that is what we are calling *series*. A theme may be as short as two words (provided one is a subject and one a verb) or as long as thirty words. This "elevator pitch" is not distortion or marketing but central to the work of blueprinting your book. Not only does

your book have to be about one thing, but you have to be able to
say what that one thing is.

**Unity** Unity is the ultimate goal of any piece of writing. It cannot
be achieved, however, by trying to be comprehensive. No matter
how hard you try, you will never completely cover your topic—
all you can do is be consistent, be coherent, and establish continuity. Unity is enhanced by careful attention to detail, limitation
of extraneous subject matter, and a vista on the way your series
interact such as can be provided by a powerful theme.

**Variation** *See* REPETITION/VARIATION.

**White Space** Also known as a *space break* or a *crot*, white space is
just that—empty space that is sometimes placed between scenes.
A fence of punctuation, such as a row of asterisks, may be used
to the same effect—separating scenes without the benefit of either a *link* or genuine *segmentation*. When your flow dries up,
you may experience the urge to put white space between scenes
instead of having to think about what material comes next. Can
you find a link instead?

**Withholding Information** When you are withholding information, it is necessary to give clues in a subtle or offhand manner
without everything "adding up." A writer withholds information
by creating distance between the iterations in a particular series.
In *suspense*, the iterations are closer together—we know there is
something we don't know, a mystery. In *surprise*, the gap between
iterations is longer so that our awareness of a particular subject
has partially faded from memory. In *shock*, the previous iteration
in the series is entirely submerged in the reader's subconscious.

# Works Cited

Andersen, Hans Christian. *Andersen's Fairy Tales.* Trans. E. V. Lucas and H. B. Paull. New York: Grosset & Dunlap, 1945.

Aristotle. *Poetics.* Trans. Malcolm Heath. New York: Penguin, 1996.

Bellow, Saul. "The Art of Fiction." *Paris Review* 36 (Winter 1966).

Campbell, Joseph. *The Hero With a Thousand Faces.* Princeton, NJ: Princeton University Press, 1949.

Catron, Louis. *The Elements of Playwriting.* Long Grove, IL: Waveland Press, 2001.

Coleridge, S. T. *Biographia Literaria.* Princeton, NJ: Princeton University Press, 1985.

*Diagnostic and Statistical Manual of Mental Disorders,* 4th ed. (DSM-IV). Washington, DC: American Psychiatric Association, 1994.

Forster, E. M. *Aspects of the Novel.* New York: Harcourt, Brace, 1927.

Freytag, Gustav. *Technique of the Drama: An Exposition of Dramatic Composition and Art.* Trans. Elias J. MacEwan. Chicago: S. C. Griggs, 1895.

Gamow, George. *One Two Three . . . Infinity: Facts and Speculations of Science.* New York: Mentor Books, 1947.

Genette, Gérard. *Narrative Discourse: An Essay in Method.* Trans. Jane E. Lewin. Ithaca, NY: Cornell University Press, 1983.

Hesse, Hermann. *Siddhartha.* Trans. Sherab Chodzin Kohn. Boston, MA: Shambhala, 2000.

Lewin, K. *Field Theory in Social Science: Selected Theoretical Papers.* Ed. D. Cartwright. New York: Harper & Row, 1951.

Longinus, *On the Sublime.* Trans. W. Hamilton Fyfe. Cambridge, MA: Harvard University Press, 1927.

Marrs, Bob. "Driving a Car at Night." WAC Faculty Resources: www.public .coe.edu/wac/IS87.htm. Accessed May 15, 2012.

Preminger, Alex, and T. V. F. Brogan, eds. *The New Princeton Encyclopedia of Poetry and Poetics.* Princeton, NJ: Princeton University Press, 1993.

Quiller-Couch, Sir Arthur. *On the Art of Writing.* New York: Capricorn Books, 1916. Reprinted 1961.

Richards, Keith. *Life.* New York: Little, Brown, 2010.

Thoreau, Henry David. "Walking." *Atlantic Monthly* 9:56 (1862).

Waugh, Evelyn. "The Art of Fiction." *Paris Review* 30 (Summer–Fall 1963).

# Acknowledgments

Books are written by authors who are people first. We good so far? That's why when we turn to this business of acknowledging, I feel like we have to acknowledge the support groups for the person before we acknowledge the support groups for the book.

My first thanks go to:

My wife, Bonnie Kane, who gave me a second chance at life from what could have been the permanent depths of addiction and despair.

My oldest daughter, Fifer—you're right there along with her. Among numerous good qualities, you make an exceptional therapist for a thirteen-year-old.

My youngest daughter, Bodhi—thank you for opening our family up to the world and teaching us that love is something you give and receive, not expect or demand.

My parents, Margot and Ellis Horwitz, well-read folk, whose sacrifices created opportunities, especially in the areas of education and exposure.

My sister, Claudia Horwitz, who started our sharing of life together by bringing letters to my crib (literally, individual cartoon characters).

Many friends and more relations, especially the RI crew: families Angell, Carey, Chase, Degnan, Dussault, Ison, Principe, and Stebenne and the inspired friendships found in Tiverton, RI: Morrow, Mullen, the Prospect Hill gang, and anyone who's ever been to a Bandoni Grill Night.

And now to the book. (And a quick prayer to the acknowledgment gods that I don't leave anybody out . . .)

People too big for any category:

Karen Byrne, my first beta reader, who cupped the flame of some very flickery drafts. She is also responsible for the kick-ass diagrams in the book.

Eve Bridburg, my literary agent, who performed the unpopular task of overhauling the book's concept, reducing the number of action steps from 81 (81! Can you imagine?) to 22. So don't complain about 22, because I can just pull out the 81 . . .

Maria Gagliano of Perigee: I'm going to ~~steal~~ adopt your manner of presenting edits and insights with an even-keeled mixture of confidence and respect.

To the Book Architecture Method (TBAM) Supergroup:

Bonnie Mioduchoski, Emma Pattee, Jaime Clegg, Jennifer Peace, Julie Matheson, Liza Ward, and Michelle Rich (by remote access). Thank you for agreeing to be living, breathing audience members and for remaining as opinionated as ever during one of my key rewrites.

The *Blueprint Your Bestseller* case studies:

Ed Bacon, Linda Fiorenzano, Lori Richardson, Jennifer Mancuso, Kimberly Hatfield, Rich Markow, and Stefan Boublil. I hope the generosity you have shown in allowing us to peek into your process is repaid to you in both your works in progress and in your life!

The *Blueprint Your Bestseller* "local color":

Bonnie Kane, Chloe Marsala, David Kingsbury, Dennis Greene, Jennifer DeLeon, Jennifer Peace, Julie Matheson, Leyla Hamedi, Sondra Levenson, Stacey LaPierre, Stephen Catania, and Wendy Dubow Polins. Your quotes, images, and stories put much of what I was thinking "into scene." Which, as we know by now, is invaluable, since scenes are the building blocks of our work, blah, blah . . .

Grub Street:

Thank you, Eve Bridburg, for founding this nonprofit writing mecca in Boston, and for connecting me with Chris Castellani. Chris, your taste for treading the edge in teaching inspired me to develop the Book Architecture Method through the unique offerings that you, Sonya Larson, named *Blueprint Your Book*! That's two-thirds of this book's title right there, yo!

Thank you, Whitney Scharer, for being Whitney Scharer and no one else. The blog at www.GrubDaily.org that Whitney edits formed an important firing range for some of this material as did www.BeyondtheMargins.com, headed by Nichole Bernier and the rest of the BTM gang.

Professional contacts (you should hire if you can):

Chloe Marsala: In the puzzle that is Book Architecture, you are an end piece. Every Ro$hi needs a Biz (lest this be an inside joke, check out the book trailer/short films on the BYB tour). Your arrival had both cosmic and comic timing.

Andrew Boardman of www.Manoverboard.com: How many web designers transcend engineer, brand manager even, and influence the very way a person looks at himself? Question's kind of moot, since I only needed one.

Chip Cheek, my copyeditor: Chip, when are you going to get that digital avatar of yourself as a cowboy lassoing words, since you're from Texas? Or is that just another one of my bad ideas you will question directly and politely?

Mariah Ashley, author photographer and sense maker during my previous incarnation in wedding planner hell.

Dave Stebenne, unpretentious genius in many visual media, you are possessed of a talent that is hard to describe; like, if you didn't know a Dave, you wouldn't have a mystical white ox wandering through your book trailer.

Rudy Vale, present at the coining of Book Architecture many years ago and remaining a source of deep reflection (aka she has a great bullshit meter).

Lisa Tener of www.LisaTener.com, who has brought many books to life and has encouraged hundreds of writers to own their power in very concrete ways.

Uncategorizable, but providing essential sustenance:

James Bowers; Jeanette Shaw of Perigee; Josie Carroll; Mel and Nat Whiteford; Ollie Kane; Ron Vale; contributors of such generous blurbs: Elizabeth Flock, Ed Bacon, Liza Ward, Nicole

Bernier, SaraKay Smullens, and Vernā Myers; and the rhythm section of Art Don't Pay: Rob Degnan and Tim Ison.

Finally, I would like to thank anyone who has read and experimented with the concepts contained in this book. Without you we got nothing.

# About the Author

STUART HORWITZ is the founder and principal of Book Architecture, a firm of independent editors based in Providence and Boston (www.BookArchitecture.com).

He developed the Book Architecture Method over fifteen years of helping writers get from first draft to final draft. In the process, those same writers have become authors: signing with top literary agencies and landing book deals at coveted publishing houses.

Book Architecture's clients have reached the bestseller list in both fiction and nonfiction, and have appeared on *The Oprah Winfrey Show*, *Today*, *The Tonight Show*, and in the most prestigious journals in their respective fields.

Horwitz holds degrees in literary aesthetics from New York University and East Asian studies from Harvard University. He is an award-winning poet and essayist who has taught writing at Grub Street of Boston and Brown University.

He lives in Rhode Island with his wife and two daughters.